THE
LONE
RANGER?

3rd Edition. Copyright 2024 to D.M. Yourtee

Historical accounting is compiled and adapted from overview writings and observations on leadership and the impact on humanity. The document is formed using guidelines for the APA method of citation

Published by Minds-Eye Manuscripts, LLC

No copyright infringement is intended regarding drawings and pictures. This work contains sections from an Anthology "The Vistavien Agenda" by D.M. Yourtee.

From the Lone Ranger

Friend, these are, indeed, your times, these times! Humanity appears to have found a mixed personality.

 Let's see. There are some who wake up each morning nicely consumed with futuristic missions. "How do I make a better surgical robot; how can I make it possible for more children to get food." Yes, there are those.

Then there are the great masses….

INTRODUCTION

A SONG

THE LONE RANGER

Sometimes I sit yeah, feeling alone
No one to talk to. I got no telephone
And at night I wake up, I just lie and stare
Come on and save me from this nightmare!

Hi ho silver, here come the lone ranger
He's riding on down to rescue me!

I know the road I must take, with a wink of my eye
I leave old friends behind like old alibi
I take all they throw against me I make a stand
For truth and justice and for the common man.

Hi ho silver, here comes the lone ranger
He's riding on down to rescue me!

And I guess it took some time for me to decide
If you were just my hero or my friend
Watching with my innocent eyes
Your silver stallion rides
across my room. I'd listen as he cried-

Hi Ho Silver!

Here comes the lone ranger
He's riding on down to rescue me!

Source: Lyric Find, As Sung, writers: Chris Parren /James Diamond (Singer)

THOUGHTS ABOUT IT

Many of us remember that promise, don't we?

As children, we envisioned someone, parent or someone would come swooping down and save us!

As adults, we have looked for, expected that there is and will be a "Lone Ranger," a hero courageous, powerful but loving, resolving problems!

And we have hoped, you know, the country's leaders, a president, a caring politician, a general, a teacher, whoever, a special someone-will save us!

In this volume, the question is asked at last.

Is there a Lone Ranger?

Who has been one, or most importantly, who will be the one to save the rest of us!

MEETINGS IN THE PARK

City Park. Beautiful little lake down from a tree-studded hill. There a most handsome man sits on a bench much in the shade. Sitting on some cushions on the grass up close and looking up at him is Triestan and his aunt, Andrea.

They made a habit of coming up the hill to see him, at least a couple of times a week, because they had become friends. After all, he rescued Triestan from near-drowning in the lake when he went out too far to get his little sailing ship.

The Man was always full of information. And they began to view him not as a rescuer but as a friend and much like a teacher.

Today as they sat and enjoyed the quiet beauty of the lake with the occasional drifting, shading clouds, he had turned on a bit of a radio playing soft music; when switching channels, it came on full of rhythm!

"So, you heard that song," he asks Triestan, who with his aunt were doing some rhythmic bouncing?

Andrea jumped in first full of excitement! "Oh yes, and it made me remember the shows-radio then TV him with Tonto. And Triestan added a very sure expression on his face; that song was about him from the comics. But I heard Jim Diamond wrote it about his dad, who would always come to help him. The Lone Ranger could solve anything!

Then, Triestan asked, "Was the Lone Ranger really any good?"

Andrea said, you see, sweetheart, the Lone Ranger always solved problems for people completely. He was very caring. There was always a perfect ending to each story.

From Triestan, still, I always wondered. Is he real, I mean here, alive? Is he still here? Has that been on the minds of other people? I mean, over time and always. Then both looked up to The Man on the bench. Can you tell us about him, please!

Looking at them fondly, The Man said, ok, but the familiar story was a western time in America. Your question requires looking into much more earth time.

And so, for several days (with apologies each time), he opened a notebook on his lap and read to them. Here, following, in order is what he read.

BEGINNINGS

After looking up to The Man, Triestan said, "So who is the Lone Ranger, or I guess should be called the Lone Ranger?

Response: Well, let us look deeper back in time.

First, what are humans? We are much like animals, with the essential brain, some limbs for locomotion, eating, defecating, urinating, surviving, and driven by feelings copulating, then promulgating more of the same and some variants. Until the species, bipedal, with thumbs, we as "Homo sapiens" began in numbers. But there is a marker of a time when this hero first could have appeared.

Human evolution was the lengthy process of change by which people originated from those apelike ancestors. Scientific evidence shows that all people's physical and behavioral traits originated from apelike ancestors and evolved over approximately six million years. Simple drives still drove those earliest. Needing to eat and driven to hunt, they indeed grappled hopefully day by day loosely together to survive. Even so, the matter is much more profound because we did not just crudely exist over the millennia.

As Homo sapiens came out of the soup, they must have had those that took charge for others, needing self to survive! Of course, the most successful, the first Lone Ranger, we do not know, being genuinely mysterious, but that "person" had to be there, or we would not be.

Even so, where was that first Lone Ranger most likely?

Well, Humans first evolved in Africa, and much of our human evolution occurred on that continent. The fossils of early humans who lived between 2 and 6 million years ago come entirely from Africa.

The change that led to a deliberate "Ranger Acting Person" occurred most likely when the Ranger moved his "Tribe" out of Africa and went into the rest of the world!

There are many estimates as to this time. However, it was probably somewhat later than the usual estimates of around 2 million years ago.

We know this by what seems like rather curious evidence. *That is why and when humans began to wear clothing!*

Principal investigator David Reed, the Associate Curator of Mammals at the Florida Museum of Natural History on the University of Florida campus, made the linking observation. He did this by studying lice in modern humans to understand human evolution and migration patterns better. His latest five-year study used DNA sequencing to calculate when clothing lice first began to diverge genetically from human head lice.

Once, a human uncomfortable with the arid climate dobbed mud, straw, and leftover animal hide and thus clothed-showed others and with them led the long trek to Europe and the rest of the world to a better climate.

It seems, thus, as the climate so shifted, and backed by the lice evidence, humans migrated out of Africa about 60,000 years ago, according to such new paleoclimate research. And there is more to this.

 "Clothes" would mark the beginning of self-evidence, what we are in any recognizable way, and those (as may seem absorbed) who so covered themselves and led others to new worlds would be the very earliest truly recognizable, Lone Rangers.

This is saying, as it must be, the first Lone Rangers began some time about 60,000 years ago (see the picture). As needed by the American Lone Ranger, a unique individual costume was worn by the Lone Rangers from the beginning!

 Yes, the lone ranger began when the human had an intense self-reflective personality.

That aspect may have been the primary "seed." But well before the *sapiens,* there was Homo *habilis.* Homo habilis, or "handyman," lived about 1.4 million years ago in Eastern and Southern Africa. Homo habilis had a bigger brain and was more in sync with our human evolutionary tree. Both species were about

4.5 to 5.5 feet tall, and their lifespan was likely about 30 to 40 years. However, for habilis, "It was a very much more stressful life because they were in continual competition with carnivores for their food. So, that predecessor was a creator of the early carved hunting weapons, although they lacked the defined creativity of the Homo sapiens. That weapon aspect had to be evolved in our first Lone Ranger, who recognized belonging to others, needing to care for them realized in addition to clothing there was a weapon should it be needed to hunt or defend.

In short, the first Lone Ranger was most likely a "clothed" individual who felt "personality" and caring for others. This Homo sapiens is likely the one who leads "Humankind" out of Africa into northern (cooler) climates.

Triestan entered with you said, "led." What about that business of leading? The Lone Ranger certainly had to feel leadership.

And Andrea added, "that opens a question of some importance in identifying the Lone Ranger. Would the Rangers not have a needed, a specific kind of "leadership in personality?" Oh yes, that would be absolute!

 From The Man, yes, good point, which is critical to consider finding the Lone Ranger.

To dig into that next time, we are together; I will first tell you what a Lone Ranger should not be!

Triestan commented; let's do that now; I want to know! Andrea entered, "Yes, me too, Tris. We want to continue, but its' time to go on to your "Regular School."

ANTI-LONE RANGERS

Together again, the next day, The Man comments, "In our history, there have been too many who folks thought were Lone Rangers, but who turned out rather horrible."

And to start, he reads from an article by Jan-Benedict Steenkamp., Author of "Time to Lead: Lessons for Today's Leaders from Bold Decisions That Changed History," Published Oct 29, 2020.

The 20th century is the most violent in history. It had more than its "fair" share of utterly evil leaders. Here are my top 10.

#1. Adolf Hitler\

Any list of evilness invariably is topped by German Chancellor and *Führer* Adolf Hitler, who came to power (democratically!) in January 1933. His mad quest for revenge, conquest, and ethnic cleansing nearly succeeded. In December 1941, nearly all of Europe was under his heel. After Stalingrad, though, the Third Reich lost battle after battle, and in May 1945, after Hitler committed suicide, Germany unconditionally surrendered. The country lay in ruins, six million Jews were murdered, and World War II mourned 55 million dead. Hate, racism, xenophobia, and megalomania are but a few words to describe this man.

#2. Mao Zedong (1893-1976)

Mao was a successful guerrilla fighter against the Japanese invaders and the corrupt Kuomintang government of Generalissimo Chiang Kai-shek. In 1949, he had overcome them all, and the People's Republic of China was proclaimed. It went downhill ever after. In the purges of the early 1950s, millions of "wealthy" peasants, intellectuals, and "saboteurs" were killed. Then came the "Great Leap Forward" (1958-1962), one of the most insane experiments in social engineering ever. Private plots were abolished, and communal kitchens were introduced. It was a disaster. Production plummeted, and the ensuing "Great Chinese Famine" cost the lives of up to 45 million people. Not having had enough, a few years later, the dictator launched the "Great Proletarian Cultural Revolution" in 1966. Millions of people were persecuted and suffered public humiliation, arbitrary imprisonment, torture, hard labor, and execution. When Mao died in 1976, the country's per capita income was lower than Congo's, and China had lost over 55 million lives. Not that Mao cared. Purity above everything else--his purity, absolutely no compassion.

#3 Joseph Stalin (1878-1953)

In any list of evil men, Soviet dictator Joseph Stalin ranks high. He rose to power in the 1920s, after the death of Lenin. A succession of Five-Year programs industrialized the country but at unimaginable human costs. This, and forced collectivization of agriculture, led to widespread famine, which cost the lives of countless millions. Then came the "Great Terror," involving purge after purge of the party apparatus and society. Millions were sent to forced labor camps, their death, or both; the death rate in the Gulags was horrific. Almost all senior Red Army officers were purged before Hitler attacked, ensuring the dismal performance and the horrific losses in the early stages of World War II. In the early 1950s, he was planning another bloody terror, but thankfully he died before he could unleash it upon the harried nation.

#4 Pol Pot (1925-1998)

Pol Pot was the leader of the Communist Khmer Rouge. He grabbed power in Cambodia in 1975 and set about to create a communist paradise on earth. Not surprisingly, it was worse than Dante's Seventh Circle of Hell (violence). To fulfill his vision of an agricultural society, the urban population was forcibly relocated to the countryside to work in collective farms. Money was abolished, and all citizens were made to wear the same drab black clothing, which made Mao costumes look fashionable. Intellectuals were summarily murdered—this included people who wore glasses. This experiment in social engineering cost about 25 % of the population's lives and was immortalized in the Hollywood movie *Killing Fields*. His evil government was toppled after four years by invading Vietnamese forces.

#5 Leopold II (1835-1909)

The Belgian King Leopold II was a nasty piece of work. He deserves inclusion in this list by what happened in Congo, which he acquired as his private property in 1885 in the Berlin Conference when much of Africa was divided among European powers. From the beginning, he was in it for the money, extracting maximum the amount of wealth from this vast colony. Millions of Congolese inhabitants, including children, were mutilated, killed, or died from disease during his rule. Failure to meet rubber collection quotas was punishable by death. Forced labor was instituted to increase production. Around 10 million people died during his brutal regime in Congo. Not that he cared. Things got so bad that in 1908, he was forced to hand over the colony to the Belgian state.

#6 Kim Il-Sung (1912-1994)

Kim Il-Sung was the dictator of North Korea from 1949 till his death in 1994. The official name of North Korea is the "Democratic People's Republic of Korea." All of it is a lie. There is nothing democratic about North Korea. The people are treated as slaves, and it is not a republic but a de facto kingdom with leadership going from father to son. Kim invaded South Korea in 1950, and in this war, some 3 million people perished, including 12-15% of North Korea's population. Subsequent Stalinist economic policies and widespread repression led to poverty and famine in which hundreds of thousands, if not millions, died. Sadly, the country has not improved much under his son and grandson, both of whom are utterly ruthless, evil leaders in their own right. What a family!

#7. Saddam Hussein (1937-2006)

Saddam Hussein was president of Iraq from 1979 to 2003. The common thread in his life was his morbid thirst for power, absolute power, no matter how high the cost in human blood. Saddam was notable for using terror against his people, including mustard and nerve gas, to subdue the Kurds. He attacked Iran in 1980. Having learned nothing, he invaded Kuwait in 1990, leading the First Gulf War, and another 85,000 dead. The war ended in a stalemate and one million dead. Uprisings after the war led to the death of over 150,000 civilians. The list goes on until he was toppled in 2003 by American and Allied forces and hanged in 2006. Good riddance.

#8 Idi Amin (1925-2003)

Idi Amin ruled as dictator of Uganda after launching a military coup in 1971. His nickname is "Butcher of Uganda." Amin's behavior steadily worsened during the 1970s. He expelled all Asians and handed over their businesses to his cronies, which led to a collapse of the economy. Yet, the Asians were "lucky" compared to his violent persecution of rival Uganda tribes killed by tens of thousands. The total death toll of his regime amounted to half a million out of a population of 10 million. He was feared for feeding victims alive to crocodiles. He boasted that he kept the decapitated heads of political enemies in his freezer, although he said that human flesh was generally "too salty" for his taste. His megalomania knew no limits. Among his titles were "Lord of All the Beasts of the Earth and Fishes of the Seas" and "Conqueror of the British Empire in Africa." He was deposed in 1979 and fled to Saudi Arabia. He never expressed any remorse for his brutal deeds. He, too, was the subject of a Hollywood movie, *Last King of Scotland.*

#9 Mengistu Haile Mariam (1937-)

Mengistu Haile Mariam rose to power in 1977 as a member of the murderous Derg regime in Ethiopia, which had toppled and murdered Emperor Haile Selassie in 1974. His policies were to modernize Ethiopia's economy along Leninist-Stalinist-Maoist lines. Land, companies, banks, etc., were all nationalized. Farmers were compelled to join collectives. The free market was abolished. Not surprisingly, it was a disaster. People resisted, famine ensued, and economic deprivation was widespread. This did not stop Mengistu. Widespread resistance was met with brutal force. Between 1 and 2 million people were killed during his regime. According to the *Times*, it was not uncommon to see students, suspected government critics, or rebel sympathizers hanging from lampposts each morning. Mengistu himself is alleged to have murdered opponents by garroting or shooting them, saying that he led by example. Yes, we need such examples. Human Rights Watch describes his regime as "one of the most systematic uses of mass murder by a state ever witnessed in Africa." After the collapse of the Soviet Union, his position became untenable, and he fled the country.

#10. Josef Mengele (1911-1979)

No list of 20th-century evil leaders is complete without Josef Mengele's, whose nickname *Todesengel* ("Angel of Death") says enough. He was the most prominent medical doctor at the Auschwitz death camp (concentration camp seems too friendly a term). He selected victims to be killed in the gas chambers and happily administered the gas himself. That is bad enough, but what earned him his place in this top-ten of infamy is his experimentation on humans. Mengele used Auschwitz as an opportunity to continue his research into genetics and heredity. He was fascinated by twins. The experiments he performed on twins included amputation of limbs, intentionally infecting one twin with typhus or some other disease and transfusing that twin's blood into the other. He experimented with changing eye color, including injecting chemicals into the eyes of living subjects. And so on. Mengele has become the stereotype for the mad scientist for whom ethical boundaries were a nuisance, who would do anything to satisfy their lust for knowledge. Unfortunately, he was never captured.

Obviously, Jan-Benedict Steenkamp has provided us descriptions of some of the Anti-Lone Rangers. However, before describing exemplary leadership, there is a record in history that must be shown. That is what the Lone Rangers overtime had to deal with in their lonely "Riding on Downs."

If you can come tomorrow, I will read through that.

WHAT LONE RANGERS
MIGHT HAVE TRIED TO FIX

Andrea and Triestan arrived a bit later than usual; Triestan's sister Grace had a Teacher-Parent Conference.

Now sitting with The Man", he began to read on the matter of wars between humans. He read from an article by Raymond C. Kelly on the "Question of Armed Conflict." According to the cultural anthropologist and ethnographer Raymond C. Kelly, the earliest hunter-gatherer societies of *Homo erectus* population density was probably low enough to avoid armed conflict. The development of the throwing-spear and ambush hunting techniques made potential violence between hunting parties very costly, dictating cooperation and maintenance of low population densities to prevent competition for resources. This behavior may have accelerated the migration out of Africa.

Raymond believes that this period of "Paleolithic war-lessness" persisted until after the appearance of *Homo sapiens* ending only at the occurrence of economic and social shifts associated with sedentism[1] when new conditions incentivized organized raiding of settlements.

That drive, creating an additional need to survive, produced a rise of the more beast-like human and a fundamental challenge for a Lone Ranger. How serious was this?

~~~~~~~~~~~~~~~~~~~

In cultural anthropology, sedentism (sometimes called sedentariness) is the practice of living in one place for a long timc. Essentially, sedentism means living in groups permanently in one place.
~~~~~~~~~~~~~~~~~~~

Of The Many cave paintings of the Upper Paleolithic, none depicts people attacking other people explicitly. Still, there are depictions of human beings pierced with arrows both of the Aurignacian-Périgordian (roughly 30,000 years old) and the early Magdalenian (c.17,000 years old). This possibly represents "spontaneous confrontations over game resources" in which hostile trespassers were killed; however, other interpretations, including capital punishment, human sacrifice, assassination, or systemic warfare, cannot be ruled out.

Skeletal and artifactual evidence of intergroup violence between Paleolithic nomadic foragers is absent as well

At the site of Nataruk in Turkana, Kenya, numerous 10,000-year-old human remains were found with possible evidence of major traumatic injuries, including obsidian bladelets embedded in the skeletons, that should have been lethal. According to the original study, published in January 2016, the region was a "fertile lakeshore landscape sustaining a substantial population of hunter-gatherers" where pottery had been found, suggesting storage of food and sedentism. The initial report concluded that the bodies at Nataruk were not interred but were preserved in the positions the individuals had died at the edge of a lagoon. However, evidence of blunt-force cranial trauma and lack of internment has been called into question, casting doubt upon the assertion that the site represents early intragroup violence.

However, the oldest rock art depicting violence between hunter-gatherers in Northern Australia has been tentatively dated to 10,000 years ago.

The earliest, limited evidence for war in Mesolithic Europe likewise dates to ca. 10,000 years ago, and episodes of warfare appear to remain "localized and temporarily restricted" during the Late Mesolithic to Early Neolithic Cave painting of a battle between archers, Morella la Vella, Spain.

Indeed, Iberian cave art of the Mesolithic shows explicit scenes of battle between groups of archers. A group of three archers encircled by four is found in Cova del Roure, Morella la Vella, Castellón, Valencia. A depiction of a  more significant battle (which may, however, date to the early Neolithic), in which seventeen running archers attack elven archers, is found in Les Dogue, Ares del Maestrat, Castellón, Valencia. At Val del Charco del Agua Amarga, Alcañiz, Aragon, seven archers with plumes on. Such early war was influenced by the development of bows, maces, and slings. The bow seems to have been an essential weapon in early warfare in that it enabled attacks to be launched with far less risk to the attacker when compared to the risk involved in mêlée combat. While there are no cave paintings of battles between men armed with clubs, the development of the bow is concurrent with the first known depictions of organized warfare consisting of clear illustrations of two or more groups of men attacking each other. These figures are arrayed in lines and columns with a distinctly garbed leader at the front. Some paintings even portray still-recognizable tactics like flanking and envelopments. Their heads are fleeing a group of eight archers running in pursuit.

Such Systemic warfare appears to have been a direct consequence of sedentism as it developed in the wake of the Neolithic Revolution.

An essential and clear example is the massacre of Talheim Death Pit (near Heilbronn, Germany), dated right on the cusp of the beginning

European Neolithic, at 5500 BC. Investigation of the Neolithic skeletons found in the Talheim Death pit in Germany suggests that prehistoric people from neighboring tribes were prepared to brutally fight and kill each other to capture and secure women.

Researchers discovered that there were women among the immigrant skeletons, but there were only men and children within the local group of skeletons. They concluded that the absence of women among the local skeletons meant that they were regarded as somehow unique; thus, they were spared execution and captured instead. The capture of women may have indeed been the primary motive for the fierce conflict between the men.

Well, that was a detailed tracing, of which I was unaware. But clearly, we did begin to kill each other even early in the time of Home sapiens. Even so, Andrea asked The Man how bad has that been in more recent times?

Responding, with many pages from a report in hand, he read the record, which seemed as if it unfolded that it arose in an almost storm-sounding repetition! Then as he went on, it indeed was appropriately surrounded by Thunder from impending weather.

Following is the report he read.

There are military records that tell the story. However, please note these numbers do not tell of the millions of civilians (non-combatants) killed.

Here I read from a list, giving date, conflict, and the number of killings.

The following are after religious leader Zoroaster's benevolent propositions.

549 BC–530 BC Conquests of Cyrus the Great.100,000+

499 BC–449BC Greco–Persian Wars300,000+

343 BC–290 BC Samnite Wars 33,500+,

336 BC–323 BC Wars of Alexander the Great 142,000+

264 BC–146 BC Punic Wars 1,250,000–1,850,000

264 BC–241 BC First Punic War 400,000+

218 BC–201 BC Second Punic War 770,000+

149 BC–146 BC Third Punic War 150,000–250,000

262 BC–261 BC Kalinga War (India)150,000–200,000

230 BC–221 BC Qin's Wars of Unification   700,000+

58 BC–50 BC Gallic Wars   1,000,000

These are Post the Propositions of Moses and Christ.

A.D. 60–61 Iceni Revolt 150,000+

A.D.66–136   Jewish–Roman   Wars   1,270,000-2,000,000 Roman attempt to permanently root out Judaism

A.D. 115–117 Kitos War440,000+– Part of Jewish–Roman Wars

A.D. 132–136 Bar Kokhba Revolt 580,000 the Third Jewish-Roman War

A.D. 269 Gothic War (269)   320,000+

A.D. 277 Probus's German War 400,000+

A.D. 376–382 Gothic War 40,000+

A.D. 184–280 3 Kingdoms War 40,000,000 Wei vs. Shu vs. Wu China

A.D. 184–205 Yellow Turban Rebellion 3,000,000–7,000,000

A.D. 304–439 Wars of the Sixteen Kingdoms 150,000+ Chinese States

A.D. 395–453 Hunnic Reclaims 165,000+

A.D. 534–548 Moorish Wars 5,000,000+

A.D. 629–1050 Arab–Byzantine Wars 130,000+

A.D. 711–1492 Reconquista 7-10,000,000

A.D 598-614 Goguryeo Kingdom-Sui Dynasty War 300,000+

A.D. 755–763 An -Shi Rebellion 700,000+

A.D. 993–1019 Goryeo Korea–Khitan Empire Wars 90,000+

A.D. 1075–1077 Lý–Song Empire vs. Dai Viet (Nam) War 600,000+
A.D. 1095–1291 Crusades 1,000,000–3,000,000 (Originally Byzantine
Empire vs. Seljuq Empire but evolved into Christians vs. Muslims.)

By now, most major religions established.

A.D. 1208–1229 Cathar Crusade (Papal vs. Cathar) 200,000–1,000,000

A.D. 1206–1368 Mongol conquests of Eurasians 30,000,000–40,000,000*

Excludes the (up to) 200,000,000 deaths from the Black Death migration

that may have been associated with the Mongol expansion

A.D. 1296–1357 Wars of Scottish Ind. from England 60,000-150,000

A.D. 1337–1453 Hundred Years' War 2,300,000–3,300,000

A.D. 1370–1405 Conquests of Timur Empire 8,000,000–20,000,000

A.D. 1455–1487 Wars of the Roses   35,000–50,000

Following are "Modern Wars," naming only those with a death toll >25,000

 A.D. 1494–1559 Italian Wars (Great Wars of Italy) 300,000–400,000

A.D. 1519–1632 Spanish conquest of the Aztec Empire 2,300,000+

A.D. 1519–1595 Spanish conquest of Yucatán 1,460,000+

A.D. 1533–1572 Spanish conquest of the Inca Empire 8,400,000+

Deaths from Spanish conquests include disease transferred from Europe

~~~~~~~~~~~~

Note: Medieval wars-500years of intermittent war. The identity of individual wars is not specific. "Reconquista" Spanish-Portuguese vs. Muslim states (711–1492, 781 years) "Muslim conquests in India" (12th to 16th c., 500 years) "Crusades" (ten or more campaigns during the period 1095–1291, 196 years), "Mongol conquests" (1206–1368, 162 years), "early Muslim conquests" (622–750, 128 years), "Hundred Years' War" (1337–1453, 115 years).
~~~~~~~~~~~~

A.D. 1521–1566 Campaigns of Suleiman the Magnificent   200,000+

A.D.1524–1525 German Peasants vs. Swabian Leage100,000+

A.D. 1562–1598 French Wars of Religion (Huguenot) 2,000,000–4,000,000

A.D. 1568–1648 Dutch War of Independence 600,000–700,000

A.D. 1585–1604 Anglo-Spanish War 138,285+

A.D. 1592–1598 Japanese invasions of Korea 1,000,000+

A.D. 1616–1683 Transition from Ming to Qing 25,000,000+

A.D. 1618–1648 Thirty Years' War   4,000,000–12,000,000

A.D. 1635–1659 Franco-Spanish War (1635–59) 200,000+

A.D. 1639–1651 British Civil Wars- Three Kingdoms 876,000+

A.D. 1642–1651 English Civil War   356,000–735,000

A.D. 1658-1707 Mughal–Maratha Wars 5,000,000+

A.D. 1672–1678 Franco-Dutch War 220,000+

A.D. 1683–1699 Great Turkish War 380,000+

A.D. 1700–1721 Great Northern War 350,000+

A.D. 1701–1714 War of the Spanish Succession 400,000–1,250,000

A.D. 1741–1751Maratha expeditions in Bengal 400,000+

A.D. 1756–1763 Seven Years' War   868,000–1,400,000

A.D. 1765–1769 Sino-Burmese War (1765–69) 70,000+

A.D. 1771–1802 Tây Sơn rebellion 1,200,000–2,000,000+

A.D. 1775–1783 American Revolutionary War 37,324+

A.D. 1798–1801 French campaign in Egypt and Syria 65,000+

A.D. 1802–1803 Saint-Domingue expedition 135,000+

A.D. 1803–1815 Napoleonic Wars 3,500,000–7,000,000

A.D. 1812 French invasion of Russia 540,000+

A.D. 1808–1833 Spanish American Wars of Independence 600,000+

A.D. 1810–1823 Venezuelan War of Independence 228,000+

A.D. 815–1840 Mfecane -South Africa Ethnic 1,500,000–2,000,000

A.D. 1820–1876 Carlist Insurgents (Spain)Wars 200,000+

A.D. 1821–1831 Greek War of Independence 170,000+

A.D. 1830–1903 French conquest of Algeria 480,000–1,000,000

A.D. 1850–1864 Taiping Rebellion 20,000,000–70,000,000

A.D. 1853–1856 Crimean War 356,000–410,000 One of 1st wider uses rifles

A.D. 1854-1873 Miao Rebellion 4,900,000

A.D. 1855-1868 Punti–Hakka Clan Wars 500,000-1,000,000+

A.D. 1856–1873 Panthay Rebellion   890,000–1,000,000

A.D. 1857–1858 Indian 1st War Independence 800,000–1,000,000

A.D. 1861–1865 American Civil War 650,000–1,000,000

A.D. 1862–1877 (China) Dungan Revolt 8,000,000–20,000,000

A.D. 1862–1867 French intervention in Mexico 49,287+

A.D. 1864–1870 Paraguayan War 300,000–1,200,000

A.D. 1868–1878 Ten Years' War-Spain vs. Cuba 241,000+

A.D. 1870s–1884 Argentina vs. Mapuche people 30,000–35,000

A.D. 1873–1914 Infidel War Netherlands /. Aceh Sultanate 97,000–107,000

A.D. 1894–1895 First Sino–Japanese War 48,311+

A.D. 1895–1898 Cuban War of Independence (US-Cuba vs. Spain)362,000+

A.D. 1899–1902 thousand Days' War 120,000+

A.D. 1899-1902 South African War (Second Boer War) 73,000–90,000

A.D. 1899–1912 Philippine–American War 234,000+

A.D. 1910–1920 Mexican Revolution 500,000–2,000,000

A.D. 1912–1913 Balkan Wars 140,000+

A.D. 1914–1918 World War I 16,000,000–40,000,000+

A.D. 1917–1922 Russian Civil War   5,000,000–9,000,000

A.D. 1918–present Kurdish separatism in Iran 15,000-58,000

A.D. 1918–2003 Iraqi–Kurdish conflict 138,800–320,100

A.D. 1921–present Kurdish rebellions in Turkey 100,000+

A.D. 1923–1932 Second Italo-Senussi War (Libya) 40,000+

A.D. 1927–1949 Chinese Civil War 8,000,000–11,692,000

A.D. 1932–1935 Chaco War-Bolivia vs. Paraguay 85,000–130,000

A.D. 1935–1936 Second Italo-Ethiopian War 278,000+ (Maj. Ethiopian)

A.D. 1936–1939 Spanish Civil War 500,000–1,000,000

A.D. 1937–1945 Second Sino-Japanese War 20,000,000–25,000,000

A.D. 1939–1945 World War II 56,125,000–85,000,000

The largest and deadliest war in history

A.D. 1939–1940 Finland vs. Soviet Union-Winter War 153,736–194,837 A.D.
1940–1941 Greco-Italian War27,000+ Part of World War II

A.D. 1941–1944 Continuation War 387,300+ Part of World War II

A.D. 1945 Soviet–Japanese War 33,420–95,768 Part of World War II

A.D. 1946–1954 First Indochina War 400,000+

A.D. 1946–1949 Greek Civil War 158,000+

A.D. 1947–1948 France vs. Malagasy Insurgents 11,342–89,000

A.D. 1948–1958 La Violencia Conflict 192,700–194,700

A.D. 1948–present Internal conflicts in Myanmar   130,000–250,000

A.D. 1948–present Arab–Israeli conflict 116,074+

A.D. 1948-1949 Indian annexation of Hyderabad 29,000–242,000

A.D. 1950–1953 Korean War 1,500,000–4,500,000

A.D. 1954–1962 Algerian War of Independence 400,000–1,500,000

A.D. 1954–present India and Myanmar vs. Naga People 34,000+

A.D. 1955–1975 Vietnam War 1,300,000–4,300,000

A.D. 1955–1972 First Sudanese Civil War   500,000+

A.D. 1960–1965 Congo Crisis USA/Belgium vs. Simba Rebels 100,000+ A.D. 1961–1974 Angolan War of Independence 83,000–103,000

A.D. 1962–1970 North Yemen Civil War 100,000–200,000

A.D. 1964–1974 Mozambican War of Independence 63,500–88,500

A.D. 1964–present Insurgency in Northeast India   25,000+

A.D. 1964–present Colombian conflict vs. Far Left and Right 220,000+

A.D. 1967–1970 Nigerian Civil War 1,000,000–3,000,000

A.D. 1969–2019 Moro Conflict- the Philippines vs. Jihadist 120,000+

A.D. 1969–present Communist rebellion in the Philippines 30,000–43,000

A.D.1 971   Bangladesh War of Independence 300,000–3,000,000+

A.D. 1974–1991 Ethiopian Civil War 500,000–1,500,000

A.D. 1975–2002 Angolan Civil War 504,158+

A.D. 1975–1990 Lebanese Civil War 120,000–150,000

A.D. 1975–2007 Insurgency in Laos 100,000+

A.D. 1978–2021 War in Afghanistan 1,240,000–2,000,000 A.D.

A.D. 1978–present Kurdish–Turkish conflict 45,000+

A.D. 1979–1989 Soviet–Afghan War 600,000–2,000,000

A.D. 1979-1992 Salvadoran Civil War 70,000–80,000

A.D. 1980–1988 Iran–Iraq War 289,000–1,100,000

A.D. 1980–present Internal conflict in Peru   70,000+

A.D. 1981–1986 Ugandan Bush War 100,000–500,000

A.D. 1983–2005 Second Sudanese Civil War 1,000,000–2,000,000

A.D. 1983–2009 Sri Lankan Civil War 80,000–100,000

A.D. 1986–present Somali Civil War 300,000–500,000

A.D. 1987–present Lord's Resistance Army insurgency 100,000–500,000

A.D. 1988–present Artsakh Liberation War - pending

A.D. 1990–1991 Gulf War   25,500–40,500

A.D. 1991–2002 Algerian Civil War 44,000–200,000

A.D. 1991–1995 Bosnian War 97,000–105,000

A.D. 1991- Iraqi vs. Rebels (Civil War) 85,000–235,000

A.D. 1991–2002 Sierra Leone Civil War 50,000–300,000

A.D. 1993–2005 Burundian Civil War (vs. Hutu rebels) 300,000+

A.D. April–July 1994 Rwandan genocide 800,000

A.D. 1998–2003 2ndCongo or Great War of Africa   2,500,000–5,400,000

A.D. 1999–2003 Ituri conflict (part 2nd Congo War) 60,000+

A.D. 2001–present? Global War on Terrorism 272,000–1,260,000

A.D. 2001–present? War in Afghanistan 47,000–62,000

A.D. 2003–2011 Iraq War -2nd Gulf War 405,000–654,965

A.D. 2003–present War in Darfur 300,000+

A.D. 2004–present Kivu Conflict– Part 2nd Congo War 100,000+

A.D. 2004–2017 War USA, UK vs. Terrorist N/W Pakistan 45,900–79,000

A.D. 2006–present Mexican Drug War 150,000–250,000

A.D. 2009–present Boko Haram insurgency Nigeria 51,567+

2,400,000 internally displaced

A.D. 2011–present Syrian Civil War   387,000–593,000+

A.D. 2013–present Rojava-Islamist conflict 50,000+

100,000[123] Syrian Kurds fleeing to Turkey

A.D. 2014–2017 Iraqi Civil War (2014–2017) 195,000–200,000+

A.D. 2014–present Yemeni Civil War 233,000+

So, billions of people were murdered following the bellicose drive of leaders acting on pressures on their location, violent impulses, "narcissistic drive," and the missing sense of empathy for people," just happening," and indeed accepted.

Even so, in short- day to day- were Lone Rangers present? Did they have others to support them?

Then, The Man continued in this "Non-Lone Ranger Discourse." While the forgoing must be cited, the individual day-to-day insanities over time should also be noted. Of course, it would take book after book to report all of these sometimes ridiculous and, more often, cataclysmic leader misleading's. So, the following gives examples of which many are unaware—witness these examples, from the millions where a Lone Ranger was missing.

The dictator of Russia in 1962, Nikita Khrushchev, called Chairman Mao of China an "old boot" (for his toughness), but the Chinese word for boot also means prostitute. Mao thought he was being called an old whore, which started the split between China and Russia. If you will causing killing conflicts in their other places of influence, the checks and balances of invested interest by either in those places out of collaborative control.

World Wat II killed millions of people and put millions into poverty (see the wars section). The rise of Adolf Hitler and his postulates should have been a deep concern for the leader of every nation. However, Britain and France were far less concerned about Hitler's remilitarization of Germany than they should have been. The Fuhrer intended to expand his country's borders, and he did so with little resistance. Going against the Versailles Treaty that ended World War I, Germany annexed Austria in 1931. Franco-British apathy encouraged Hitler to go further, seeking to take over a part of Czechoslovakia called the Sudetenland. Britain and France signed the Munich Agreement with Germany to keep a lid on potential conflict, granting the territory to the Third Reich!

Subsequently, British Prime Minister Neville Chamberlain triumphantly returned to London, proclaiming "Peace in Our Time." Then, German tanks rolled into Poland in September 1939, and a total tragic killing war began lasting until 1945, Neville did your leadership lack a bit of long-range forethought? Well, there was peace for another eleven months, anyway.

"To reflect is one thing, but to regret is another. Regret is useless". said, Idris Elba

Somewhat valid point. We can regret all we want thinking about the vast record of inhumanity from humans. However, purely regretting this with no action is of no help. Hence, are cited the following examples.

Empress Wu, Born A.D. 624, high-level concubine to Emperor Taizong, was called "Charming Lady," should have been called the "Witch of China." She s gave the emperor two sons for succession, then had a daughter. She strangled that child to death so she would have no successor. Eventually, the Emperor had her elevated to Empress. In that role, she ordered the resisters as "murderers", had their hands and feet cut off then had them drowned. This was her practice for the rest of her reign.

Ersabet Bathory was born into nobility in Hungary A.D. 1560 was a sadistic serial murderer who was reported to have tortured and killed up to 650 women aided by her children's wet nurse, a dwarflike manservant, and a brawny woman thought to be a witch. She tortured peasant girls for entertainment by lashing and bludgeoning them to death. She bathed in the blood of virgins to maintain her skin in a youthful appearance. There were so many other atrocities in her record that it is inappropriate here to relate them. As victims were peasants, the ruling class relatives turned a blind eye to her atrocities. None of them were Lone Rangers! When she turned attention to a few royals, the king had her tired, to which, as royalty, she could not be convicted. Eventually, she was walled up in her castle until four years later, she died. Of course, we can't call this king of Hungary a lone ranger, as his other record belies that title.

And to select another from the millions of examples, human empathy is lost. Delphine LaLaurie of New Orleans married a dentist in 1825. She lived in luxury in a fine home in the French Quarter and outwardly appeared a great hostess to marvelous parties. However, one night a neighbor noticed a servant jump to death out of a third-story window. Authorities discovered that this resulted in her mistress chasing her, and authorities fined her $300 and had servants auctioned off to the highest bidder. She repurchased them. Later, when a fire broke out in 1834, the firemen discovered slaves chained to stoves (who set fire to bring attention), pleaded for the firemen to look in the attic. There they discovered a dozen naked bodies, dead and alive, chained to walls and onto operating tables. One man had a hole cut in his head with a stick inserted into his brain. One woman had her cut-off arms reattached to resemble a crab, and body parts were scattered everywhere. The Dr. was no Lone Ranger, denying he knew of his wife's "activities," and she escaped later to die in Paris (never punished)

Yes, any original lone rangers who may have existed, as humans began to behave in mass, had terrible challenges. In fact, in every city, in all the world, there were and remain today senseless, horrible murders taking away from us, even the children of the future.

Even so, we need not go on and on. This failing happens again not only at the individual level, but it also stems out from the top.

Consider, for example, the action of the President of the United States of America (for four years to 2020), who buried in his wealth, his narcissism and desire to maintain political power, stimulated far-right actions, causing killing in the streets and even an attack on the capital when fearing to lose the election. Which he did and with his selfish persistence in the 'Big Lie "left the political parties and many in the country at odds hampering recovery from a Pandemic and International Relations.

Reflect deeply! Each human being, born from an ape-like structure, embedded in the needs of self, hunger, need to urinate, defecate, etc., has over time been self-driven to survive no matter the consequences. Humans from primitive tribes carried animal killing instinct into an unforgiven killing of other humans in other tribes. Many lacked the compass of species recognition, concern for others. Without remorse, without empathy, there resulted in war after war, horrible cruelty repeatedly, and the death and suffering of billions.

In so doing, they followed without using their sense of caring for those who demanded and commanded such actions, not recognizing their own intellect to say NO!

Even so, among each group, there were a few who tried to define more humane ways. These were the early Lone Rangers, and they were those who so often had to stand alone. Indeed, what was inside of these individuals was a guiding intelligence born within the survival instinct, an understanding of the needs of all humanity through intelligent and empathetic leadership.

What are those qualities, those that must be within every Lone Ranger? An example is presented next, a general guide, but one that reveals some important markers.

A LONE RANGER'S SUBSTANCE

The next day the scene repeated as Andrea and Triestan arrived, and on their cushions sat for another reading by The Man on the bench.

I am sure that you have noted my references of late, that we are attempting to identify not one but all Lone Rangers. Well, they must work to lead. Any true Lone Ranger would have excellent leadership qualities and drive.

Andrea put in, well indeed, as we have seen and learned well, the Lone Ranger should not be a narcissist or one only with self-interest.

For that matter, do humans naturally have leaders? Or is leadership unexpected in our biology?

Well, as much as many of us hate to admit it, most of us are naturally predisposed to seek the guidance of leaders. The dynamic between leaders and followers can be found across countless species– from horses to bees to wolves.

Then, do we need leaders?

Leaders should indeed help us to identify, understand and refine our purpose. They should help us to align our thoughts and clarify the reasons behind our life and work. Humans seek answers and understanding to everything they do, and leaders should go some way to support this need.

But there is a "catch twenty-two" in this, isn't there. Should not the leader have a profound interest in our true welfare? And further, how do leaders happen? Are leaders made?

Research by psychologists has proved that leaders are 'mostly made! The best estimates offered by research is that leadership is about one-third born and two-thirds made. The fact that leadership is mainly made, to be honest, is mixed news for the benefit of most of us. Folks do have to work to be leaders, but it is not impossible and, of course, very desirable. In fact, superior upbringing with self-sufficiency gained can produce many more with the necessary internal characteristics.

Nonetheless, what would happen if we didn't have leaders?

The short answer is that the world could collapse into sheer chaos, and anarchy would be everywhere. Humankind is still dependent on the pack. Without strong leaders within our pack that help us understand the world, stand for us, and tell us what to do, we do not know what to do like the pack.

Can a group exist without a leader?

Leaders build the values and behaviors of a team. Without a leader, there isn't a standard to follow, and team integrity eventually erodes. Since integrity is such a critical element of leadership, it makes sense that the values and team integrity could erode without a stellar leader's presence.

Then how would such a leader arise?

From where do leaders come?

In reality, most leaders have a combination of personal attributes, family background, education, professional and personal networks that help us understand why they, rather than their peers, took on a leadership role. However, there is no reason anyone cannot be a leader once they have a rational upbringing.

Brian Tracey has pointed out the characteristics of poor leaders, those with Non-Lone Ranger identities.

It's a known fact that, for the most part, objective-oriented groups (workforces in Brian's terms) are only as capable as their leader. However, not everyone has the good fortune to work under an inspiring, capable, and motivating leader. Whether you are working under a leader or employing a leader, it's essential to learn how to recognize the qualities of a bad leader and act accordingly! Outlined below are a few telltale leadership qualities to look for that those poor leaders often demonstrate.

1. Poor Integrity

One of my favorite leadership quotes is, "Integrity is the most valuable and respected quality of leadership. <u>Always keep your word</u>." It doesn't matter how capable, intelligent or effective a leader is. If they lack *moral integrity*, troubles are bound to follow. For one, folks look to their leaders for examples of what behavior is acceptable. If a leader is engaging in unethical behavior, it won't be long before the people around them engage in unethical behavior. Sooner or later, a lack of moral integrity almost always leads to a person's undoing, which is why it should be a significant red flag!

2. Lack of Adaptability

Great leaders know how to employ a range of leadership styles. That depends on what is needed in the situation. The simple truth is that not all people are motivated by the same factors, and there is no "one-size-fits-all" approach that will work in every situation.

Good leaders recognize this and are fluid, while <u>poor leaders may be stuck in their ways and unwilling to adapt</u> to the needs in the situation.

If you notice that a leader is stubborn, slow to adapt to changing situations, and demonstrates a "my-way-or-the-highway" attitude, they are likely a poor leader.

3. Little Vision for The Future

The job of a leader is to push forward, and good leaders should always be focused on how they can make tomorrow more efficient and productive than today, as demonstrated by Elon Musk's vision of the future. Bad leaders, though, often get complacent and stay satisfied with the status quo. If a leader is not focused on the future and demonstrates a clear plan for continuously improving, progress is unlikely to happen.

4. Lack of Accountability

The best leaders take accountability when things go wrong and give credit to others when things go right. People want to know that they follow a leader who will give them due credit when they do well and not throw them under the bus when things go wrong. However, some leaders cannot shoulder this responsibility and instead deflect blame to others and take credit for themselves. In the end, this behavior is going to do very little to motivate people to succeed.

5. Poor Communication Skills

Excellent communication skills are one of the most essential traits for a leader to have. It doesn't matter how effective a plan a leader can draw up. If they cannot communicate that plan to their employees easily to understand and motivate, little progress will be made. A good leader needs to be able to listen intently and communicate clearly. If a leader demonstrates an inability to communicate their ideas and expectations to others, they are not likely to be a very effective leader.

Leadership can make or break any activity, indeed the reputation of being considered a Lone Ranger. Remember that great leaders must regularly demonstrate integrity, adaptability, vision, accountability, and communication skills to effectively lead those needing help to success. As we seek the Lone Ranger, these criteria should always be at the forefront!

Some discussion and review then occurred. In that, Triestan asked his aunt why The Man has pointed this out to us?

She said he had shown us the horror that results from leaders who are not Lone Rangers, and now I think he is trying to put us into a path showing what leaders would be and who would be a Lone Ranger.

Leaving for School, Triestan asked, "After the first Lone Rangers, did more Rangers arrive or ever evolve?"

The Man said as they left the park, "Well, there is a record." Next, we will identify some of them, ones we can unmask!

Thus, over the next ten days, The Man presented information on persons who acted in some way as Lone Rangers. They were in order, Lone Rangers of Behavior, Benevolent Ruler Lone Rangers, Lone Rangers That Tried to Save Millions of Humans, Lone Rangers of Ideals, and Lone Rangers of Invention.

LONE RANGERS Of BEHAVIOR

Listing of wars and insane actions, of course, tells of horrible human suffering. Wars entered to reverse some perceived anomaly only produced reason to continue one way or another, war thus never seeming to end on planet earth.

So again, together with The Man on the bench, the two were all ears as he read, opening new insights. To help, as he always did, he prefaced his reading with an introduction focusing on the topic (and showing a table).

Faiths Developed	Years Available*
Hinduism	4000
Zoroastrianism	3000
Judaism	2650
Buddhism	2560
Confucianism	2500
Christianism	2040
Jainism	>2000
Taoism	1560
Islamism	1378
Shintoism	1300
Sikhism	500
Baha'ism	138
Humanism	82
*Each of these had a Leader at Inception, a possible Lone Ranger	

Benevolence: The Man then began with a forward comment. As we discussed, leadership must be the case for the Lone Ranger, with a compassionate outcome in mind. We have learned over much of our history that there have been attempts to lay down morality and love for all to practice. Some of those proposing made them into "faiths."

We could call those developing these ideas (they being truly alone) Lone Rangers, specifically in interpersonal practices. The Man then pointed out the faiths, how long they had existed, and noted the Ranger proposing each.

He then continued. Among the earliest beliefs leading to faith and fundamental benevolence was Zoroaster, who ultimately preached that it is based upon a vision as others from a divine recognition.

According to Zoroastrian belief, when Zoroaster was 30 years old, he went into the Daiti river to draw water for a Haoma ceremony. When he emerged, he received a vision from one "Vohu Manah."

Vohu Manah took him to another six spirits, later called "Amesha Spentas," where he received the completion of his vision.

This vision radically transformed his view of the world and all else to come. Because Zoroaster came to believe as one of the first in one creator God, he tried to teach this view to others.

He taught that only one God was worthy of worship! Although in the Jewish faith, there is a belief on the time axis of this centering even before Zoroaster, this is quite possibly, the first complex statement of that to center a faith that captures vast hordes of humans.

Furthermore, to attract a wide following, who knew and suffered from some of the deities of the old religion - the Deavas who appeared to delight in war and strife. Zoroaster said that these were evil spirits and were workers of "Angra Mainyu," God's adversary.

And, indeed, Zoroaster's ideas lingered at first; he only had one convert his cousin Maidhyoimanha! Of course, the basic one-God idea set off great controversy. And as we see in so many monotheistic starts, the local religious authorities opposed his ideas. They felt their faiths, power, and rituals were threatened because Zoroaster taught against over-ritualizing religious ceremonies. And a great many ordinary people did not like Zoroaster's downgrading of Daeva to an evil spirit.

So, after twelve years, Zoroaster left his home to find somewhere more open for new ideas. In this is implanted the saga of an early faith that we find in other faiths, the exodus of the Prophet, one who, no matter the suffering, stood alone.

Nonetheless, as it turns out, he finally found a place of acceptance in the country of a King in Bactria known as "Vishtaspa." This is on the eastern periphery of the Iranian world, now part of Afghanistan.

The King and his queen, named Hutosa, heard Zoroaster debating with the religious leaders of his land and decided to accept Zoroaster's ideas and make them the official religion of their kingdom! So, it was somewhat fulfilled Zoroaster died; it is believed peacefully, in his late 70s.

Zoroastrianism still exists, and although it has not survived entirely uniform, it has no overt conflict with any other faith but is exclusive in and of itself. There remain many religious centers, and even worldwide, although it is now a minor sect among the 12 major faiths.

As seems to be the case, perhaps too often, modern era influences significantly impact individual and local beliefs, practices, values, and vocabulary, sometimes complementing tradition and enriching it, but sometimes also displacing tradition entirely.

Still, there is a central theme. Zoroastrians believe that there is one universal and transcendent God, "Ahura Mazda". He is said to be the one uncreated Creator to whom all worship is ultimately directed.

The religion states that active participation in life through good thoughts, good words, and good deeds is necessary to ensure happiness and keep chaos at bay. This active participation is a central element in Zoroaster's concept of free will, and Zoroastrianism rejects all forms of monasticism or withdrawal from life (as do the monks). The faithful believe that Ahura Mazda will ultimately prevail over the evil Angra Mainyu or Ahriman, at which point the universe will undergo a cosmic renovation, and time will end.

In Zoroastrian tradition, life is a temporary state in which a mortal is expected to participate in the continuing battle between truth and falsehood actively.

Zoroastrianism is often compared with "Manichaeism," a religious doctrine based on the separation of matter and spirit and good and evil that originated in 3rd-century Persia and combined Zoroastrianism and Buddhism elements and Gnosticism, which is nominally an Iranian religion but has its origins in the Middle-East.

On the other hand, Zoroastrianism rejects every form of asceticism, has no dualism of matter and spirit (only good and evil), and sees the spiritual world as not very different from the natural one. The word "paradise" (via Latin and Greek from Avestan pairi-daeza, literally "stone-bounded enclosure") applies equally to both. Manichaeism's fundamental doctrine was that the world and all corporeal bodies were constructed from the substance of Satan. This is an idea that is fundamentally at odds with the Zoroastrian notion of a world that God created, all good, and any corruption of it is an effect of the bad. The main that people hearing this over time was surely killing others is contradictory to the foundational ideas of the faith.

The first wars between humans occurred about 5500 B.C. That is, people were killing each other in horrible, brutal mass murder ways almost 4000years before Zoroaster. The Hindus are closest to truncating the practice of mass murder but were still about a thousand years short. We have had about 3000years of Zoriasterism. He lived and preached somewhere between 1500B.C and 500 B. C. So, with about A.D. 2000, add about 1000 to make Zoriasterism. That is, the faith was present in later wars, but its impact was minimal.

It was up to Judaism, Muslimism, or Christianity to stop the practices of cruelty and mass murder. That is the benevolent precepts developed by the Lone Rangers Moses, Mohmed, and Jesus Christ. And from Christ came a type of new covenant.

Indeed, Christ messaged through his disciples became the Mediator, High Priest, and God himself manifest in flesh form who "took away all our sins." This Lone Ranger's new covenant did give His commandments which are

Just like the ten commandments or the fundamental ancient law from Moses, there are commandments from Jesus Christ, as these following.

1. Love the Lord your God with all your Heart and Soul
2. Believe that Jesus is in your Father
3. *Do not be angry with your brother without a cause*
4. *Love one another*
5. *Pray for your Enemies*
6. Repent
7. Go and Make Disciples

Apart from these commandments, He also taught various mysteries through his parables that people are expected to follow.

The peaceful and loving ideas brought forward by the prophecies presented above have led to some peace on earth, the beginnings of a drive toward humanness.

Yet, they do not record saving all people; indeed, that record of death associated with the faiths is very troubling. There certainly have been atrocities in the presence of religious wars and killing, misrepresenting fundamental ideas. A selection on that topic is presented later in this volume.

To dare to propose the ideals of benevolence and forgiveness as occurred is, of course, a prime mark of the Lone Ranger. As history unfolds, the ideas are diluted, requiring, it seems, new Lone Rangers to help humankind out of the mess.

The following sections address that, i.e., identifying Lone Rangers in different objectives (as noted forgoing).

BENEVOLENT RULER LONE RANGERS

On this day, The Man addressed through his readings that some in history have tried what we expect is imbedded in the Lone Ranger. That is, individuals have tried solutions in rescues that end with the "Good for All. "

Should this not be the programs of rulers. Well, six have tried. Here to start is the account of those Lone Rangers who are the six most benevolent rulers in History.

 When you turn the pages of history, you can find many strong and famous kings and rulers who left their mark. These are known as benevolent rulers.

This account reveals six of such famous benevolent rulers of history who are brave and kind-hearted. These kings and rulers are known for their power, strength, and welfare schemes and policies introduced to improve lives. Here following is a look into these great rulers of legendary history.

1) Suleiman I of the Ottoman Empire
November 6, 1494, to September 7, 1566
Suleiman was the longest reigning king of the Ottoman Empire. In his 69 years of rule, he worked extensively to maintain law and order in the kingdom. He also encompassed most parts of the Middle East, Southeastern Europe, and Rhodes. Moreover, he made education free for every child by opening many schools and educational centers throughout the empire.

2) James I of England
November 6, 1494, to September 7, 1566

He was the first emperor who ruled over England and Scotland together. Under his rule, literature and the fine arts flourished as he allocated special funds for them. He also made many reforms for the welfare of women and children. During this period, the British East India Company expanded its business worldwide through sea routes.

3) Augustus of Rome

January 16, 27 BC to August 19, AD 14

Augustus Caesar was one of the best emperors in the history of Rome. He was famous for his diplomatic policies that were focused on peaceful coexistence with the neighboring states. He also made a significant contribution to the field of military reforms. Moreover, he is remembered as the founder of some of the most beautiful cities of Italy, such as Verona, Rome, Bella Napoli, etc.

4) Victoria of the United Kingdom

June 20, 1837, to January 22, 1901

Queen Victoria ruled the British monarch for 67 years. During her reign, the British Empire expanded to encompass most parts of Africa, Asia, and North America. The United Kingdom flourished under her reign, and it was during this period, many scientific and cultural reforms took place throughout the world.

5) Louis XIV of France

May 14, 1643, to September 1, 1715

Under his reign, France became the most powerful country in Europe by extending its territory to the neighboring states. He ended the socially inculcated feudalism in France and modernized the country. During this time, the fine arts flourished. And he also made developments in the field of infrastructure by making roads, hospitals, bridges, guest houses, etc.

6)Meiji of Japan

February 3, 1867, to July 30, 1912

He became the Emperor of Japan at the age of 14. But even in his teenage years, he was quite mature in his making administrative decisions and policies. Due to his contribution to science and technology, Japan emerged as an industrial powerhouse by the end of the nineteenth century. The Japanese still revere him.

Those above were some of the best leaders in world history. Although their power was immense and could have been used without regard for human life, what made these leaders famous are their philanthropic policies focused solely on the prosperity and well-being of their citizens. They exercised, it could be said, significant aspects of good leadership.

Per the song, we guess it takes some time for us to decide if they were just our heroes or just our friend. Good was done; perhaps there were a few other Lone Rangers to help secure the ideas.

Some more examples of Lone Rangers in particular types follow

LONE RANGERS THAT TRIED
TO SAVE MILLIONS OF OTHER HUMANS

It is possible as one reviews history to find those that exhibited the fundamental drive of the Lone Ranger, which is caring intensely for others.

Stanislav Petrov. On September 26, 1983, he was the duty officer at the  command center for the Oko nuclear early-warning system. The system reported that a missile was being launched from the United States. Petrov judged the report to be a false alarm. His decision is credited with preventing an incorrect retaliatory nuclear attack on the United States and its NATO allies, resulting in a large-scale nuclear war. An investigation later confirmed that the satellite warning system had indeed malfunctioned.

Maurice Ralph Hilleman (August 30, 1919-April 11, 2005). He was an  American microbiologist specializing in vaccinology and developed over 36 vaccines, more than any other scientist. Of the 14 vaccines routinely recommended in current vaccine schedules, he developed eight: namely those for measles, mumps, hepatitis A, hepatitis B, chickenpox, meningitis, pneumonia, and also Haemophilus influenza bacteria. He also played a role in discovering the cold-producing adenoviruses, the hepatitis viruses, and the cancer-causing virus SV40. He is credited with saving more lives than any other medical scientist of the 20th century. Robert Gallo described him as "the most successful vaccinologist in history."

(This section is selected from the kindnessblog.com, June 23, 2015)

Vasili Arkhipov. Vasili was one of three officers on board a Soviet nuclear-armed submarine during the Cuban missile crisis. Trying to avoid American ships, they went too low for radio contact. As the American navy had started dropping practice depth charges to force the sub to surface, they were unsure whether war had broken out. The ship captain believed it had and wanted to launch a nuclear torpedo (as they were authorized to do with unanimous agreement among officers). Only Arkhipov disagreed, and the torpedo was never fired.

Edward Jenner FRS. (17 May 1749-26 January 1823). Edward Jenner was an English physician and scientist from Berkeley, Gloucestershire, the pioneer of the smallpox vaccine. He is often called "the father of immunology," and his work is said to have "saved more lives than the work of any other man."

Jonas Salk. In 1955, Jonas Salk invented the polio vaccine. *He chose not to*

patent it because he only wanted to help humanity. As a result, he missed out on earning an estimated $7 billion. His sole focus was to develop a safe and effective vaccine as rapidly as possible, with no interest in personal profit.

Norman Borlaug. (March 25, 1914 – September 12, 2009)' Norman Borlaug

was an American biologist, humanitarian, and Nobel laureate who has been called "the father of the Green Revolution," "agriculture's greatest spokesperson," and "The Man Who Saved a Billion Lives." During the mid-20th century, Borlaug introduced high-yield wheat varieties combined with modern agricultural production techniques to Mexico, Pakistan, and India. Between

1965 and 1970, wheat yields nearly doubled in Pakistan and India, significantly improving the food security in those nations. These collective increases in yield have been labeled the Green Revolution, and Borlaug is often credited with saving over a billion people worldwide from starvation.

Boris Yeltsin. Thankfully, Boris Yeltsin decided to wait just a bit longer  before launching a nuclear strike against the United States. A team of Norwegian and American scientists launched a Black Brant XII four-stage sounding rocket from the Andøya Rocket Range off the northwestern coast of Norway carrying scientific equipment to study the aurora borealis over Svalbarda. It flew on a high northbound trajectory from Minuteman-III nuclear missile silos in North Dakota, all the way to the Russian capital city of Moscow. During its flight, the rocket resembled a U.S. Navy submarine-launched Trident missile. As a result, Russian nuclear forces were put on high alert, and the nuclear weapons command suitcase was brought to Russian president Boris Yeltsin. He then had to decide whether to launch a nuclear barrage against the United States. He decided against it, but Yeltsin did activate his "nuclear keys" for the first time- the first and only incident where any nuclear weapons state had its nuclear suitcases activated and ready for launching an attack.

Alan Turing. If Alan Turing had not cracked the Enigma code when he did,  Germany would have continued destroying the allied navy and may have won the second world war. The Germans were working on a nuclear program and rockets to deliver them as far as New York. It has been suggested that if anyone saved the world in the modern era, it might have been him. Unfortunately, for his efforts, he was chemically castrated (for being gay) and died of cyanide poisoning at 41.

Alexei Ananenko, Valeri Bezpalov, and Boris Baranov. These three men likely saved most of Europe from becoming a radioactive wasteland. During the Chernobyl disaster, no one was warned about the radiation for nearly two days, as those at the top were desperate to cover themselves "panic is worse than radiation." All the plant workers and firefighters fought bravely to put the fire out, none of them were told the dangers, but even when it became apparent, they went on! After the explosion, thousands of gallons of water were pumped into reactor 4 in a futile attempt to extinguish the fire. This could lead to a massive thermal explosion which would have made hundreds of square miles uninhabitable for hundreds of years and made the death toll even more prominent worldwide. Once the threat of the second explosion was confirmed, they began thousands of runs in helicopters, dumping bags of mostly sand into the exposed core. The water needed to be drained! Volunteers were called for; the slight difference here was that they were told the risk straight off. All who were asked volunteered. Valeri Bezpalov and Alexei Ananenko were selected because they knew where to go and precisely what to do. After some time, underwater in extra thick diving suits, each of the volunteers made it back to the surface, where their colleagues were jumping for joy upon hearing the news that they had managed to pen the valves. However, all three men were already suffering from radiation sickness and died later outside the power plant.

James Harrison. Specifically, his blood contains an extremely rare enzyme that can be used to treat babies dying of Rhesus disease. If you've never heard of that disease and figure, it is not a big deal; well, wait for the numbers. Being a generous type, Harrison has donated his rare, life-saving blood roughly 1,000 times over 56 years. This has saved the lives of–seriously, you're not going to believe this–over two million babies around the world.

Joseph Lister. He is often considered to be the father of modern antiseptic techniques. He was the first surgeon to suggest that doctors were transferring a disease-causing agent to women during childbirth, causing many women to die of postpartum infections. At the time, it was not unheard of for a surgeon to touch a patient or cadaver then attend to another patient without washing his hands. The idea that doctors might be making their patients sick was initially considered to be so ridiculous that Lister was treated with contempt. However, as the germ theory of disease became more widely accepted, Lister's techniques were proven to be prudent and effective at reducing disease transmission. Although we mainly remember him for Listerine today, his work has probably saved millions of lives.

Fritz Haber. Fritz Haber (9 December 1868 – 29 January 1934) was a German

chemist of Jewish origin who received the Nobel Prize in Chemistry in 1918 for his development for synthesizing ammonia, important for fertilizers and explosives. The food production for half the world's current population depends on this method for producing fertilizer.

Well, it speaks for itself. The above represent the many Lone Rangers, who were working with complex objectives, managed to achieve their goal, and in some cases lost their lives doing so. That their efforts were essentially singular does, of course, have a message about Lone Ranger-ism.

THE LONE RANGERS OF IDEALS

The thrust of history attests to attempts by some to raise humankind to a better self-being. Equally, however, the pathway to here shows us the failure to recognize the narcissistic individual who plays on our base emotions, thus accomplishing unimaginable horrors involving innocent and helpless people.

Throughout this contradictory history, a few courageous souls have seen it. That is, they have raised the importance of all of us, and they, each with their skills and insight, have created essential compliments to our existence through their idealisms.

It was never easy to create a list of the most inspiring leaders who have redefined leadership in idealism. One of the reasons this is somewhat an impossible task is because inspiration comes in many forms and has many faces.

Some leaders became great because of how they persevered with a dream despite their circumstances, only to go on and achieve such extraordinary things that they continue to be revered long after their deaths.

Others stuck by their values and protested for the rights of others, even when it jeopardized their own freedom, not to mention their lives.

Some leaders are genuinely inspirational and well-respected because of their natural flair to innovate, empower and influence others to act in meaningful ways and ultimately change the world.

Thus, the list of ten below isn't exhaustive by any means. But it indeed contains some of the most influential leaders who have shaped the world for the better and inspired positive changes among millions, if not billions.

 1. Mahatma Gandhi-The Anti-War Activist with a Global Legacy. Mahatma Gandhi left his mark on the world in more ways than one. The leader of India's independence movement achieved remarkable feats through a form of non-violent civil disobedience that would inspire millions around the world, including many of the other people on this list.

World leaders, scientists, philosophers, and even entrepreneurs have drawn inspiration from Gandhi, whose spiritual significance was just as profound as his role in liberating India.

Gandhi was born in India in 1869, a country that was then part of the British Empire. His youth was perhaps uncharacteristic of Gandhi the history books remember. After an arranged marriage at the age of 13, Gandhi rebelled against his profoundly religious upbringing by smoking, eating meat, and even stealing. By age 18, he set sail to London to study law.

A fledgling law career in India would eventually send the 24-year-old Gandhi to South Africa. It was here that he witnessed the deep-seated discrimination and racial segregation of South African society.

Perhaps the most significant turning point in young Gandhi's life occurred on June 7, 1893, where a white man threw him off a train station after refusing to move to the back of the car. That would prove to be Gandhi's first, but certainly not last, act of civil disobedience.

By 1906, Gandhi had organized his first mass civil disobedience campaign in South Africa. He would spend the next nine years fighting for Indian rights in the country before returning home to fight for Indian liberation.

Over the years, Gandhi would become a leading figure in the liberation movement. After years of struggle and multiple arrests, Gandhi's "Quit India" movement in 1942 paved the way for Britain's eventual withdrawal from the country.

Although a pacifist, Gandhi was murdered by a Hindu extremist who resented the leader's tolerance of Muslims following the declaration of Indian independence. A semiautomatic pistol at point-blank range killed a man who had spent his life preaching nonviolence.

Gandhi is today remembered for his commitment to pacifism, peaceful protest, and simple living. He single-handedly inspired millions of people to take action, preaching a message of love, tolerance, and avoiding greed.

For those reasons, he inspired civil rights movements from Apartheid South Africa to the United States and is today remembered as one of the most outstanding leaders of the 20th century.

2. Winston Churchill - Resolute Leadership During One of The Most Painful Episodes in Human History.

Winston Churchill is long remembered as one of the most outstanding leaders in modern history and the savior of democracy.

He was tasked with the daunting task of leading Britain and the Allied powers to victory against the Nazis during the Second World War. His wisdom, upright character, and persistence led Britain from the brink of defeat to victory in the most brutal war of the 20th century.

Winston Churchill was born to an aristocratic family in 1874 and served in the British military. He would go on to become a prolific writer before entering into politics. Churchill became British Prime Minister in 1940 during the height of the Second World War.

His long political career is also remembered for its persistence. It took Churchill a staggering 40 years to finally become Prime Minister. But when he finally took the helm, he became arguably the greatest leader of the 20th century.

He was not only instrumental in working with the United States and Russia to defeat the Axis powers, but he also helped establish the post-war peace that would lead the western world through one of its most significant periods of prosperity.

Churchill's leadership style would prove so decisive that he would be elected Prime Minister again in 1951.

Among Churchill's greatest strengths was his power of oratory, which helped him connect with an entire nation. His life was filled with memorable quotes that leaders to this day use for inspiration. Phrases like "We will never surrender," "The Iron Curtain," and "This was their finest hour" have withstood the test of time. Among his many honors include a Nobel Prize for Literature, and he is the first person to become an honorary US citizen.

Churchill's inspirational leadership style is especially notable when considering his bitter struggle with depression – the so-called "black dog" of his existence. In fact, historians attribute many of Churchill's successes to his ability to use his manic depression and bipolar personality to his advantage. These are just some of the reasons that make Winston Churchill truly special.

The following Churchill quote still serves as a powerful motivational nudge to stick with all our convictions even when the going gets tough:

"Never give in. Never give in. Never, never, never, never – in nothing, great or small, large or petty – never give in, except to convictions of honor and good sense. Never yield to force. Never yield to the apparently overwhelming might of the enemy."

Now we know why they called Winston Churchill "The Bulldog."

3. Martin Luther King Jr.- Celebrated Civil Rights Activist That Forever Changed America

"I have a dream that my four children will one day live in a nation where they will not be judged by the color of their skin but by the content of their character."- Martin Luther King Jr

Very few Americans are celebrated as Martin Luther King Jr., the Baptist minister, and social activist. He led the Civil Rights Movement in the United States until his tragic death in 1968.

As an African American born in the rural south in 1929, MLK faced an uphill battle all his life. Growing up in Atlanta, Georgia, the young Martin was considered a precocious student who paid little attention to his studies and found significant religious discomfort.

That all began to change in his junior year when he took a Bible class and renewed his faith. By 1948, he had earned a degree from Morehouse College before moving on to the Crozer Theological Seminary in Pennsylvania. It was at Morehouse College that MLK opened his eyes to racial inequality.

Following years of successful civil rights activism, MLK and 61 other activists founded the Southern Christian Leadership Conference in 1957.

Two years later, MLK visited Mahatma Gandhi's birthplace in India, which encouraged him to continue down the path of peaceful activism.

On August 28, 1963, MLK would leave his mark on American history by delivering the famous "I Have a Dream" speech during the March on Washington for Jobs and Freedom.

King had such a profound impact on American race relations that his efforts resulted in the passage of the Civil Rights Act of 1964, which authorized the federal government to desegregate public accommodations. The same year, MLK received the Nobel Peace Prize.

MLK would continue his activism until his assassination on April 4, 1968. His killer, James Earl Ray, was eventually apprehended after a two-month manhunt.

King's assassination was a tragic end to a remarkable life with a seismic impact on an entire nation. He proved, just like Gandhi, that non-violent protests can influence tremendous change. MLK gave his life to the civil rights movement. Nearly 50 years after his death, his legacy is stronger than ever. The third Monday of every January is Martin Luther King Jr. Day, an observed federal holiday in the United States.

4. Nelson Mandela-A Man Whose Cause for Freedom Proved Triumphant

Very few individuals personify dedication and patience like Nelson Mandela, South Africa's first democratically elected President. Getting there was a story so epic that it was made into a Hollywood biopic in 2013. Much like Martin Luther King, Jr., Mandela was one of the great transformative civil rights leaders of the 20TH century.

He not only directed peaceful demonstrations against the deeply racist South African government, but he also went on to claim the Nobel Prize in 1993 for helping to end apartheid.

Mandela was neither a politician nor an opportunist, but a man deeply committed to improving the lives of his people and applying the same message of freedom and equality to all nations.

"I hate race discrimination most intensely and in all its manifestations. I have fought it all during my life; I fight it now and will do so until the end of my days."

Born in 1918, Mandela became involved in the civil rights movement as a young man and spent 20 years leading peaceful defiance against the apartheid government. His commitment to ending apartheid landed him and 150 others in prison in 1956 on charges of treason.

Although they were acquitted, Mandela began to recognize that an armed struggle was necessary to achieve real change. His involvement with the MK movement, an armed wing of the African National Congress (ANC), landed him back in prison in 1961 after organizing a 3-day national workers' strike.

Mandela was eventually sentenced to life in prison in 1963 for political offenses. He would spend the next 27 years in jail, where he endured cruel punishment and contracted tuberculosis.

Mandela was offered early release during that time if he renounced armed struggle – a condition he flat-out refused to consider.

It wasn't until February 11, 1990, that the now 72 years old prisoner was released under South Africa's new President, Frederik Williem de Klerk, who helped broker the deal to end apartheid.

One year later, Mandela was elected leader of the African National Congress after de Klerk also unbanned it. Mandela would become South Africa's first black president in 1994 after the country's first democratic elections.

The title of Mandela's autobiography, "Long Walk to Freedom," aptly describes his lifelong journey to ending apartheid. It's hard to think of many leaders in history who gave more to his cause than Nelson Mandela. For that reason, he is one of the most celebrated people in modern history.

Mandela died on December 5, 2013, at the age of 95.

5. Albert Einstein-Rewriting the Laws of Nature for The Betterment of Humanity

Albert Einstein is perhaps the most famous scientist of the 20th century. The prized physicist profoundly impacted our understanding of the universe, including basic concepts such as time, light, and gravity.

To this day, his work is being used to guide physicists to new frontiers, helping us to understand our significance on the grandest scale.

Born in Germany in 1879, Einstein was slightly different than all the boys. His head was a little bigger, and he hardly spoke a word, which led at least one housekeeper to label him "retarded." Little did she know, this "retarded" boy would eventually go on to reshape the world through his ideas.

By age 26, Einstein had obtained his Ph.D. The same year he published four critical papers on topics ranging from the nature of light to mass-energy equivalence.

While largely ignored at first, these papers would eventually make a tremendous contribution to the scientific community, including the universally famous $E = mc^2$ equation for mass-energy equivalence.

These papers also contained the seeds of Einstein's Theory of Relativity, one of the most revolutionary ideas in history.

Although it's impossible to pinpoint precisely the nature of Einstein's brilliance, he had all of the characteristics of a genius.

He had a vivid imagination, questioned everything, and found new ways of thinking about old problems.

He also had an unrelenting work ethic that pushed him to act even on the day of his death, where he was reportedly working on a speech for a television program.

The final picture of Einstein's office taken hours before his passing showed a man who was deeply consumed in his work right up until the very end.

In addition to his timeless quotes and a deep sense of humor, Einstein is remembered for overcoming adversity. From physical setbacks as a young boy to spending two frustrating years looking for work as a teaching assistant after graduating, Einstein's life was filled with challenges. His ability to keep a positive attitude and provoke creative thought experiments were at the center of his genius. More than 60 years after his death, the world remembers not a man who spent years working at a patent office but a man who changed the world.

 6. Abraham Lincoln-The Embodiment of Liberty and Great Emancipator of Slaves

Abraham Lincoln was more than just an American hero; he represented the dawn of a new era in human civilization based on freedom, self-government, and equality.

Lincoln was born in a log cabin in Kentucky in 1809. He knew his mother all of 9 years before she died of milk sickness at the age of 34.

Her death devastated young Abraham and further alienated him from his father. One year after his mother's death, Abraham's father married a woman who significantly impacted Abraham's life by encouraging him to read.

As one might expect, there was little time or need for formal education in the Indiana wilderness. Abraham's formal education began much later in his life and amounted to a mere 18 months.

That said, Abraham was incredibly talented. Largely self-taught, he eventually became a lawyer before getting elected to the Illinois House of Representatives in 1846. It was here that his brilliance influenced what would become the freest and most prosperous nation on earth.

Lincoln rapidly modernized the economy without sacrificing his values. By 1860, he secured the Republican Party presidential nomination and was elected president. Lincoln's victory prompted southern slave states to form the Confederate States of America.

Abraham became leader of the Union during the American Civil War. He used his power of oratory to deliver the Gettysburg Address and other powerful speeches to win over the support of the American people.

To this day, Lincoln is synonymous with the principles of liberty, democracy, equal rights, and unification.

His willingness to stand alone on issues he believed in made him one of the most beloved and memorable leaders in modern history.

His refusal to compromise on slavery and instrumental role in leading the north to victory during the Civil War made him the target of Confederate plotters and sympathizers.

Lincoln was assassinated by John Wilkes Booth, a Confederate supporter, on April 14, 1865-less than one month before the end of the Civil War.

7. St. Teresa of Calcutta (Mother Teresa)-Nobel Lauriat Determined to Ease Suffering in The World

Mother Teresa's extraordinary devotion to helping the world's poorest, most impoverished, and vulnerable people left a lasting dent in the world.

Her remarkable leadership was even powerful enough to cut across conflicts and enemy lines-a, a strength exemplified during the 1982 Siege of Beirut.

Mother Teresa managed to broker a temporary cease-fire between the Israeli army and Palestinian guerrillas to rescue 37 children trapped in a front-line hospital. Teresa then traveled through the war zone alongside Red Cross workers to evacuate the young patients.

What inspired Mother Teresa's tireless drive to help others? Born in 1910 as Anjezë Gonxhe Bojaxhiu, she grew up in present-day Macedonia. Perhaps influenced by her father's death when she was only eight years old, Mother

Teresa already decided to commit herself to religious life by the time she was twelve.

Her real journey began in 1929 when she arrived in India, where she became a nun and taught at a convent in Eastern Calcutta for several decades.

The 1943 Bengal famine, which killed a staggering 2.1 million people, was a life-changing event for Teresa and left an unshakable impression. After 20 years of teaching at the convent, she felt a "calling within a calling" and left her position as headmistress to aid the poor.

Teresa then moved into the slums, where she faced hunger, poverty, and homelessness.

Despite the lack of equipment and supplies, she found a way to open a school for poor children teaching them to read and write using sticks in the dirt.

Her efforts didn't go unnoticed. A new community soon formed around Mother Teresa, opening hospices, clinics, and orphanages throughout India. Within a few years, the mission went global.

By the 1970s, the congregation was helping orphans and those afflicted by addiction, poverty, disability, old age, and disaster worldwide. In 1979, Teresa received the Nobel Peace Prize for her work to overcome poverty and suffering.

Mother Teresa passed away in 1997, but the congregation continues to live on to this day, spreading Mother Teresa's vision and serving those in need.

In 2016, the Catholic Church recognized Mother Teresa as a saint and canonized her as St. Teresa of Calcutta for her heroic virtue.

8. Stephen Hawking-The Physicist Who Proved That Determination and Positive Thinking Can Triumph Over Even the Most Severe Limitations

Stephen Hawking probably had every reason to give up on life.

 Diagnosed with amyotrophic lateral sclerosis (ALS) at the age of 21, he would spend most of his life severely disabled to the point where he controls his communication device through the movement of his cheek muscles.

Despite his debilitating condition, Hawking became arguably the most well-known theoretical physicist since Albert Einstein. Hawking is known for his groundbreaking work on cosmology, quantum physics, and black holes.

Hawking came from humble beginnings. The eldest of 4 children, Stephen was born in England during the Second World War. By his own admission, Hawking didn't spend a lot of time studying.

That didn't stop him from graduating with full honors before pursuing a Ph.D. in cosmology at Cambridge University.

Much has been written about Hawking and his thought-provoking theories on the universe. He has received worldwide acclaim for his work and his determination to overcome a severe disability.

When he was initially diagnosed with ALS, he was given only two years to live. That was over 50 years ago. On overcoming his disability, Hawking provides this brilliant quote:

"If you are disabled, it is probably not your fault, but it is no good blaming the world or expecting it to take pity on you. One has to have a positive attitude and make the best of the situation that one finds oneself in; if one is physically disabled, one cannot afford to be psychologically disabled as well… Science is an excellent area for disabled people because it goes on mainly in the mind. Of course, most kinds of experimental work are probably ruled out for most such people, but theoretical work is almost ideal. My disabilities have not been a significant handicap in my field, which is theoretical physics. Indeed, they have helped me in a way by shielding me from lecturing and administrative work that I would otherwise have been involved in. "

Hawking's attitude comes from his sheer refusal to make excuses for his disabilities. His ex-wife Jane Hawking attributed his outlook on the world to a combination of determination and stubbornness. As Hawking clearly demonstrates, both traits have their pedigree, as does his humor and humble nature, which has been evident throughout his career. For instance, when asked what it feels like when he makes a significant scientific discovery, Hawking replied:

"I wouldn't compare it to sex, but it lasts longer."

9. Bill Gates – Entrepreneur and Philanthropist Who Inspired an Entire Generation of Innovators

Very few people are as synonymous with their industry as Bill Gates is with information technology.

It wasn't until the age of 13 that Gates saw his first computer at school. He paid to use it, and when his money ran out, he hacked into the computer to use it for free. At this point, you could say young Bill was destined for an innovative career in information technology.

Bill Gates grew up in an upper-middle-class family in Seattle, Washington, and had a very close relationship with his mother. From an early age, he showed flashes of brilliance, including a knack for business and entrepreneurship.

By the age of 15, he had already started a business with his friend Paul Allen. Little did they know that just five years later, they would be on the path to changing how the world does business and even communicates.

In 1975, Gates and Allen co-founded Microsoft. And the two poured everything they had into it. Gates' incredible vision, aggressive business strategy, and unrivaled work ethic made Microsoft the world's biggest technology company. In the process, he became incredibly wealthy.

By the time Gates and Allen decided to incorporate Microsoft in 1981, the company already had 128 employees and generated $16 million in revenue. Just two years later, the company went global.

However, it wasn't until 1985 that Gates would truly leave his mark on the world. That was the year Microsoft launched Windows, its flagship software.

For more than two decades, Gates has routinely ranked among the wealthiest people globally, and in 2016, Forbes trumped this by ranking him as the richest man in the world. But those riches didn't come without sacrifice.

Gates worked tirelessly to build Microsoft and ensure its leadership pace in an increasingly competitive market. It wasn't until 2014 that Gates stepped down as Chairman to remain active as a technology advisor.

Today, Microsoft generates nearly $100 billion annually in revenue and employs 120,000 people worldwide.

Incredibly, the founding of Microsoft isn't Gates' only legacy. As committed philanthropists, Bill and his wife Melinda Gates have established a $44 billion endowment designed to improve healthcare and reduce extreme poverty worldwide.

It is by far the most critical private foundation of its kind in the world. By 2013, Bill Gates had personally donated $28 billion to the foundation, a testament to his generosity and moral character.

10. Oprah Winfrey - Overcoming the Odds to Empower an Entire Generation of Women to Succeed.

Oprah Winfrey is much more than a television talk show host. She is one of the world's most influential business leaders who greatly influences popular culture and mainstream society.

Valued at over $3 billion, Oprah has come a long way from the rural life in Mississippi, where she was born. To say that Oprah, a black woman from the south, overcame the odds would be a vast understatement!

Very few people with her background and double-minority status would ever dream of making it in show business during the 1970s and 1980s.

Oprah's battles didn't begin with her race or gender. Her youth was filled with horrible sexual abuse at the hands of relatives and family friends.

After turbulent adolescence in the small farming community of Kosciusko, she moved to Nashville to live with her father. She would eventually enter Tennessee State University in 1971 before moving to Baltimore, Maryland, five years later to begin her career in television.

By 1986, Oprah had her own nationally syndicated television program, *Oprah Winfrey Show*. This was the platform that catapulted her to critical acclaim and global recognition.

During the 1990s, when talk shows like Jerry Springer dominated the ratings with trashy topics, Oprah promised to keep her show respectful and free of exploitive topics.

Although ratings fell initially, Oprah stuck to her guns. Oprah's integrity would lead her to more fame and prosperity over the years, as she became a mainstay in an industry filled with cheap tricks.

In addition to her television show and media celebrity, Oprah has made incredible contributions to the publishing world through Oprah's Book Club. This segment of her show promoted literacy and helped unknown authors become recognized for their work.

Her generosity didn't stop there. Through various charities, she has raised hundreds of millions of dollars to help children and underprivileged youth worldwide.

According to Forbes, Oprah was the wealthiest African American of the 20th century.

Life Magazine also recognized her as the most influential woman of her generation, a testament to this media icon who has not only done it all but inspired an entire generation of young women to pursue their dreams – regardless of their race or ethnicity.

So, there we have it. Ten inspiring leaders whose vision, perseverance, and commitment to their values helped them rise up in the face of adversity and achieve some fundamental objectives in their selected areas of interest.

Of course, these working on their own and contributing significantly to the advance of us all are indeed Lone Rangers.

LONE RANGERS OF INVENTION

Humans are an ingenious species. Though we've been on the planet for a relatively short amount of time (Earth is 4.5 billion years old), modern Homo sapiens have dreamed up and created some fantastic, sometimes far-out, things.

In far ancient history, someone bashed a rock on the ground to make the first sharp-edged tool. From the debut of the wheel to the development of Mars rovers and the Internet, many advancements stand out as particularly revolutionary.

It may seem as if we are constantly bombarded with exciting innovations and discoveries in our current times.

However, many of the new ideas and technologies shaping our modern world often can be traced back centuries in their origins. Humans have the impressive ability to keep innovating and pushing onward.

The following is a list of some of the best inventions in history, ideas, and concepts that reshaped humanity and led them into today's technological self-aggressive society.

Carefully examined, the majority have been provided by Lone Rangers of Invention, who pushed ahead for all despite doubt by others around.

~~~~~~~~~~~~~~~~~~~~

This account is selected from an article by Kashyap Vyas and Natalie Wolchover on March 03, 2016. Live Science's Jeanna Bryner contributed to this countdown, which was initially published on March 6, 2012. Jan 09, 2021
~~~~~~~~~~~~~~~~~~~~

1.The Wheel (3500 BC) – Let's Get Things Rolling: Source-https://pixabay.com-- One early invention that altered the history of humanity was the wheel. Although, the wheel is not as old as you may think. The first wheel was likely developed sometime around 4000 B.C. By that time, humans were already casting metal alloys, constructing canals and sailboats, and even designing complex musical instruments such as harps.

In fact, the key innovation was not the wheel itself, which was likely invented the first time someone saw a rock rolling along, but the combination of the wheel and a fixed axle, which allows the wheel to be connected to a stable platform. Without the fixed axel, the wheel has very limited utility.

Evidence suggests that the first device to use the wheel and axle combination was a true potter's wheel, freely spinning and had a wheel and axle mechanism. These were developed in Mesopotamia (modern-day Iraq, Kuwait, Turkey, and Syria) sometime around 4000 BCE. The oldest surviving example, which was found in Ur, dates to around 3100 BCE, and there is evidence of wheeled vehicles by the late 4th millennium BCE.

2. The Compass (c. 200 BC): Source-Theresa Thompson/Flickr--The compass has helped humans to explore and navigate around the world. In today's world of satellites and GPS, it may seem irrelevant, but it was an essential invention in its day.

However, the compass may have been initially created for spiritual purposes and only later adapted for navigational purposes. The earliest compasses were most likely invented by the Chinese around 200 BC. Some were made of lodestone, which is a naturally occurring form of mineral magnetite.

There is also evidence that other civilizations may have used lodestones for navigation or spiritual purposes. At some point, possibly around 1050 CE, people began suspending the lodestones to move freely and use them for navigation. A description of a magnetized needle and its use among sailors occurs in a European book written in 1190, so by that time, it is likely that the use of a needle as a compass was commonplace.

3. Waterwheel: Source- Smallbones/Wikimedia-- A water wheel is a machine that converts the energy of flowing or falling water into proper forms of power, such as a watermill. A water wheel consists of a wheel and several blades or buckets arranged on the outside rim forming the driving car.

The water wheel was invented independently in several places. Some of the earliest were developed by the ancient Greeks, who used it for both irrigation and milling, beginning sometime in the period between the 3rd and 1st century BC.

By at least the 1st century AD, the Eastern Han Dynasty was using horizontal water wheels for milling, and to power, the piston-bellows were used to forge iron ore into cast iron.

There are also ancient Indian texts dating to the 4th century BC that refer to devices that may have been some of the first water wheels, but this is yet to be confirmed.

4. Calendar: Source- Asmdemon/Wikimedia --The notion of a calendar, in the sense of keeping track of how many days have passed, is likely quite old — at least as old as writing itself. The first "calendars" were based on the phases of the Moon, as this would have been easy to track.

However, the lunisolar calendar, in which months are based on the lunar cycle, but years are solar — bringing the seasons into line so that, for example, the grain was harvested in the same lunar month each year — was used in the early civilizations in the Middle East and Greece. The formula may have been invented in Mesopotamia in the 3rd millennium BCE.

Many civilizations continued to use a lunar calendar, which had fewer days than the solar year. To keep the months from moving around too much, an extra month would often be added every other year. The ancient Romans used a system similar to this. Still, by around 46 BC, the system had broken down so that civic events and religious holidays were occurring during the wrong season. Julius Caesar thus introduced a new system, which set the length of the months and the year to align with the solar year. This was the Julian calendar.

This worked well but was still off by enough so that it gained a day every 128 years. To fix the error, the Gregorian calendar, which most of the world uses today, was introduced by Pope Gregory XIII in 1582.

5. Ancient Concrete: Source: Epolk/Wikimedia--We live in a world that is built using materials held together with concrete. Concrete is a composite material made from a mixture of broken stone or gravel, sand, Portland cement, and water, which can be spread or poured into molds and forms a mass resembling stone on hardening. One of the key ingredients of concrete is cement, and the origins of cement may stretch back to 3000 BC. At this time, the Egyptians were using early forms of concrete as a mortar in their building.

Around 1300 BC, builders in the Middle East were coating the outside of their clay fortresses with a thin, moist layer of burned limestone. This would chemically react with gases in the air to form a hard, protective surface. By 700 BC, the significance of hydraulic lime was known, which led to the development of mortar kilns for the construction of rubble-wall houses, concrete floors, and underground waterproof cisterns.

The ancient Greeks and Romans used a form of concrete, including Pozzolana, which uses an aluminum and silica mixture that reacts with calcium hydroxide at room temperature and water to form a substance that acts as cement. It was solid- one reason why so many Greek and Roman ruins survive today.

In 1824, Portland cement was invented by Joseph Aspdin of England. George Bartholomew laid down the first concrete street in the US in 1891, which still exists.

By the end of the 19th century, the use of steel-reinforced concrete was developed. In 1902, using steel-reinforced concrete, Auguste Perret designed and built an apartment building in Paris. This building garnered a lot of admiration and popularity for concrete and eventually influenced the development of reinforced concrete.

In 1921, Eugène Freyssinet pioneered reinforced concrete construction by building two colossal parabolic-arched airship hangars at Orly Airport in Paris.

6. Clock (725 AD) – the First Mechanical Clock: Source: Wikimedia -- Imagine modern civilization without having a sense of time? Depending on your point of view, this is either wonderful or horrible. Humans have used devices to measure time for thousands of years - the current system of time measurement, based on 60 seconds to the minute and 60 minutes to the hour, was created by the Sumerians around 2000 BC.

The earliest timepieces used the movement of the sun (sundials) or water (water-clocks). Other early "clocks" include the candle clock, the time stick, and the hourglass.

The earliest known mechanical clock used a water-powered escapement mechanism to transfer rotational energy into intermittent motion and was developed in Greece around the 3rd century BC. In the 10th century AD, Chinese engineers invented clocks that used mercury-powered escapement mechanisms, and Arabic engineers invented water clocks driven by gears and weights in the 11th century.

The first mechanical clocks that used gear trains to advance the mechanism, called a verge escapement, were invented in Europe around the start of the 14th century. These were the standard until the pendulum clock was invented in 1656.

Pendulum clocks were the most accurate timepieces until the 1930s when quartz clocks were invented, followed by atomic clocks after World War II.

7. The Printing Press: Source: Takomabibelot/Wikimedia--The printing press is a prominent part of the foundation on which modern civilization was built. German goldsmith Johannes Gutenberg is credited with inventing the printing press around 1436, although he was not the first to automate the printing process. Woodblock printing in China dates back to the 9th century, and Korean bookmakers were printing with moveable metal type around 100 years before Gutenberg.

Johannes Gutenberg's machine, however, improved on the already existing presses and introduced them to the West. By 1500, Gutenberg presses were operating throughout Western Europe, with 20 million materials, from individual pages, pamphlets, and books.

The printing press not only allowed the mass production of newspapers and pamphlets, but it also lowered the price of printed materials, making books and newspapers accessible to many, and fostering literacy.

Mark Twain described the impact of the printing press in history as, "What the world is today, good and bad, it owes to Gutenberg."

8. The Steam Engine –The Invention that Started a Revolution Source: Joost J. Bakker/Wikimedia--A Spanish mining administrator named Jerónimo de Ayanz is thought to have been the first to develop a steam engine. Hie patented a device that used steam power to propel water from mines.

However, Englishman Thomas Savery, an engineer, and inventor is usually credited with developing the first practical steam engine in 1698. His device used steam pressure to draw water from flooded mines. In developing his engine, Savery had used principles set forth by Denis Papin, a French-born British physicist who invented the pressure cooker.

In 1711, another Englishman, Thomas Newcomen, improved the steam engine. In 1781, James Watt, a Scottish instrument maker employed by Glasgow University, added a separate condenser to Newcomen's engine, which allowed the steam cylinder to be maintained at a constant temperature dramatically improving its functionality. He later developed a double rotating steam engine that, by the 1800s, would be powering trains, mills, factories, and numerous other manufacturing operations kickstarting the Industrial Revolution.

9. Vaccines – One of the Most Important Inventions for Medicine: Source: Cpl. Jackeline Perez Rivera/Wikimedia--The history of vaccination dates back farther than you might think. The practice of variolation — smearing a small cut in the skin with cowpox to give immunity to smallpox was practiced in 17th century China.

In the West, Edward Jenner is considered the founder of vaccinology after noticing that "milkmaids" often suffered from cowpox but rarely from smallpox and hypothesized that the less dangerous cowpox virus could confer some immunity to smallpox.

 In 1796, he inoculated a 13-year-old boy with cowpox, then exposed him to smallpox — demonstrating an early vaccination form.

In 1798, the first smallpox vaccine was developed.

Louis Pasteur's experiments later led to the live attenuated cholera vaccine and inactivated anthrax vaccine in humans (1897 and 1904, respectively).

In 1923, Alexander Glenny perfected a method to inactivate tetanus toxin using formaldehyde, creating a tetanus vaccine. The same method was used to develop a vaccine against diphtheria in 1926.

Viral tissue culture methods developed from 1950-1985 and led to the advent of the Salk (inactivated) polio vaccine and the Sabin (live attenuated oral) polio vaccine.

10. The Steam-Powered Train-Chugging Along with the Industrial Revolution: Source: Petar Milošević/Wikimedia--The first full-scale working railway steam locomotive was built in the United Kingdom (1804) by Richard Trevithick, a British engineer. It used high-pressure steam to drive the engine.

On 21 February 1804, the world's first steam-powered railway journey took place when Trevithick's unnamed steam locomotive hauled a train along a tramway in Wales.

The first commercially successful steam locomotive, the Salamanca, was built in 1812–13 by John Blenkinsop. In 1814, George Stephenson built a steam engine, the Locomotion No. 1, based on Blenkinsop's design.

In 1821, Stephenson was appointed as an engineer to construct Stockton and Darlington Railway in the northeast of England, which was opened as the first public steam-powered railway in 1825. His Locomotion became the first steam locomotive to haul passengers on a public railway. In 1829, he built his famous steam engine, Rocket, and the age of railways had begun.

11. Electric Battery Volta's Remarkable Feat: Source: GuidoB/Wikimedia --In the 1800s, people did not have continuous electric lines that carried a constant supply of power. So, the production of electricity was not at all an easy task.

Archaeologists have unearthed an ancient battery consisting of a clay jar filled with a vinegar solution, into which an iron rod surrounded by a copper cylinder was inserted. The battery may date back almost 2,000 years to the Parthian empire. These batteries might have been used to electroplate silver.

Alessandro Volta is generally credited with discovering the first practical battery. He invented his battery in 1799; it consisted of discs of two different metals, such as copper and zinc, separated by cardboard soaked in brine.

In 1802, William Cruickshank invented the Trough battery, an improvement on Volta's voltaic pile. Batteries had a breakthrough in 1859, with the invention of the first rechargeable battery based on lead-acid by the French physician Gaston Planté. The Nickel-Cadmium (NiCd) battery was introduced in 1899 by Waldemar Jungner.

12. Computer (1822)-The First Mechanical Computer by Babbage: Source: Victorgrigas/Wikimedia--Computers are one of humanity's greatest inventions. Initially built for doing complex mathematical calculations, bulky computers of the past have evolved into machines that sit on almost every desktop and are carried in our pockets.

Mechanical engineer Charles Babbage laid the foundation for this remarkable and most reliable invention, along with Ada Lovelace, who created the first programs. In the early 19th century, the "father of the computer" conceptualized and developed an early mechanical computer. Although there's no single inventor of the modern computer, the principle was proposed by Alan Turing in his seminal 1936 paper.

13. Refrigerator—Beating the Heat: Source: Infrogmation, New Orleans/Wikimedia--According to the report of 2009 by the U.S Department of energy, 99% of US homes have at least one refrigerator. This statistic itself is representative of the popularity of refrigerators in the modern world. The great invention helps keep perishable food products fresh much longer.

The first vapor-compression refrigerator was patented in 1835 by Jacob Perkins, based on a theory put forward earlier by Oliver Evans. British engineer James Harrison built the first mechanical refrigeration system to create ice in around 1851. He founded the Victorian Ice Works and is often called "the father of refrigeration." In 1873, he demonstrated that meat kept frozen for months remained perfectly edible.

However, the first refrigerator to be manufactured for widespread use was the General Electric "Monitor-Top" refrigerator of 1927. While it helped to rev up industrial processes initially, it became an industry itself later on.

14. Telegraph (1830-1840) – The Communication Device that Introduced the Morse Code: Source: Wikimedia--In the early 19th century, the development of the battery allowed current to be used in a controlled environment. Then, in 1820, Danish physicist Hans Christian Oersted (1777-1851) demonstrated the connection between electricity and magnetism. After this, scientists and inventors began experimenting with both batteries and electromagnetism to develop a communication system.

In the 1830s, the British team of Sir William Cooke and Sir Charles Wheatstone developed a telegraph system using magnetic needles that could be pointed around a panel of letters and numbers using an electric current. Around the same time, Samuel Morse worked to develop an electric telegraph of his own, eventually producing a single-circuit telegraph that worked by pushing the operator key down to complete the electric circuit of the battery. This sent the electric signal to a receiver at the other end.

At the same time, Morse and Alfred Vale also created what is now called Morse code to transmit messages across telegraph wires. @#

15. Steel – From Pins to the Brooklyn Bridge: Source: Wlodi/Wikimedia-- The weight to strength ratio has made steel a preferred choice of builders over other materials. For example, while Bronze was the first metal forged for use by humans, it is relatively weak. Around 1,800 BC, people along the Black Sea began using iron ore to create sturdy wrought iron weapons. The even-stronger cast iron was first made in China, beginning around 500 BC.

Around 400 BC, Indian metalworkers invented a smelting method that used a clay dish to hold ingots of the wrought iron and pieces of charcoal. When these were inserted into a furnace, the wrought iron melted and absorbed the carbon in the charcoal. When the crucibles cooled, they contained ingots of pure steel-which was much stronger and less brittle than iron.

In 1856, British engineer Henry Bessemer developed a process that blasted air through molten pig iron to create carbon-free, pure iron. The Bessemer Process paved the way for steel production, making it one of the biggest industries on the planet. Today steel is used in the creation of everything from bridges to skyscrapers.

16. Electric Bulb (1880)-Lighting Up the World: Source: William J. Hammer/Wikimedia--Electric lights were pioneered in the early 19th century by Humphry Davy. He experimented with electricity and invented an electric battery. When he connected wires between his battery and a piece of carbon, the carbon glowed, producing light. His invention was known as the electric arc lamp. Over the next seven decades, other inventors also created "lightbulbs." In 1850 an English physicist named Joseph Wilson Swan created a "light bulb" by enclosing carbonized paper filaments in an evacuated glass bulb. However, the filaments used tended to break after a few days of use, making them impractical. But without a good vacuum, his bulb had too short a lifetime for commercial use. However, in the 1870s, better vacuum pumps became available, and Swan developed a longer-lasting lightbulb.

Thomas A. Edison improved Swan's design by using metal filaments, and in 1878 and 1879, he filed patents for electric lights using different materials for the filament. He eventually discovered that a carbonized bamboo filament could last over 1200 hours. This discovery made commercially manufactured light bulbs commercially feasible.

17. The Airplane (1903) – Making the Flying Dream Come True: Source: John T. Daniels/Wikimedia--Leonardo da Vinci was one of the visionaries who believed that powered flight was possible. He made several designs for flying machines, although there is no evidence that any were constructed.

Many other flying machines were dreamed up since da Vinci's time, and powered flight was achieved thanks to the work of countless inventors over the centuries. It was the Wright Brothers who became the first people to achieve controlled, powered flight. With their work on gliders, the duo's success laid the foundation for modern aeronautical engineering by demonstrating what was possible. On December 17, 1903, Wilbur and Orville Wright achieved the first powered, sustained, and controlled flight. Now humans can cover thousands of miles in a matter of hours thanks to the achievement of Wilbur and Orville Wright.

18. Transistors (1947) – The Secret of Modern-Day Computing: Source: Unitronic/Wikimedia--The electronics age owes its inception to transistors used to amplify electric signals. These replaced the bulky vacuum tubes that came before.

In 1926, Julius Lilienfeld patented a field-effect transistor, but the working device was not feasible. In 1947 John Bardeen, Walter Brattain, and William

Shockley developed the first practical transistor device at Bell Laboratories. Their invention won the trio the 1956 Nobel Prize in physics.

Transistors have since become a fundamental piece of circuitry in countless electronic devices, including televisions, cellphones, and computers, making a remarkable impact on technology.

19. Arpanet (1969)-The Early Internet: Source: Defence Systems Agency/Wikimedia--The Internet has no single "inventor." Instead, it has evolved, created from the intelligent and inventive minds of persons who were challenged by persons "stuck in the mud." It started in the United States around the 1950s, along with the development of computers.

The first workable prototype of the Internet came in the late 1960s, with the creation of ARPANET, or the Advanced Research Projects Agency Network. By the 1970s, the Transmission Control Protocol (TCP/IP) was developed by Vinton Cerf, which enabled computers to communicate with each other. ARPANET adopted the TCP/IP protocols on January 1, 1983, and from there, researchers began to assemble the "network of networks" that became the modern Internet.

The Internet is a networking infrastructure, whereas the World Wide Web can access information using the Internet. The father of the World Wide Web is considered to be British Computer Scientist Tim Berners-Lee, who created the Web to allow information-sharing between scientists in universities and institutes around the world.

In 1989 and 1990, Berners-Lee worked with Belgian systems engineer Robert Cailliau to formalize a proposal for the web architecture, including describing a "WorldWideWeb" in which "hypertext documents" could be viewed by "browsers."

Others that have helped Us

20. The Nail: Without nails, civilization would surely crumble. This key invention dates back more than 2,000 years to the Ancient Roman period and became possible only after humans developed the ability to cast and shape metal. Previously, wood structures had to be built by interlocking adjacent boards geometrically, a much more arduous construction process.

Until the 1790s and early 1800s, hand-wrought nails were the norm, with a Lone Blacksmith heating a square iron rod and then hammering it on four sides to create a point, according to the University of Vermont. Nail-making machines came online between the 1790s and the early 1800s. Technology for crafting nails continued to advance; After Henry Bessemer developed a process to mass-produce steel from iron, the iron nails of yesteryear slowly waned. According to the University of Vermont, by 1886, 10 percent of U.S. nails were created from soft steel wire. By 1913, 90 percent of nails produced in the U.S. were steel wire.

Meanwhile, the screw, a stronger but harder-to-insert fastener, is thought to have been invented by the Greek scholar Archimedes in the third century B.C.

21. The Internal Combustion Engine: In these engines, fuel combustion releases a high-temperature gas, which, as it expands, applies a force to a piston, moving it. Thus, combustion engines convert chemical energy into mechanical work. Decades of engineering by Many Scientists went into designing the internal combustion engine, which took its (essentially) modern form in the latter half of the 19th century. The engine ushered in the Industrial

Age and enabled the invention of various machines, including cars (Henry Ford) and aircraft (Wright Brothers).

22. The Telephone: Though several inventors did pioneer work on electronic voice transmission (many of whom later filed intellectual property lawsuits when telephone use exploded), Alexander Graham Bell was the first to be awarded a patent for the electric telephone in 1876.

According to the Public Broadcasting System (PBS), he drew his inspiration from teaching the deaf and visiting his hard-of-hearing aunt, according to the Public Broadcasting System (PBS). He called the first telephone an "electrical speech machine," according to PBS.

The invention quickly took off and revolutionized global business and communication. According to PBS, when Bell died on Aug. 2, 1922, U.S. telephone service stopped for a minute to honor him.

23. Penicillin: First discovered in 1928, penicillin was being mass-produced and advertised by 1944.

It's one of the most famous discovery stories in history. In 1928, the Scottish scientist Alexander Fleming noticed a bacteria-filled Petri dish in his laboratory with its lid accidentally ajar. The sample had become contaminated with mold, and everywhere the mold was. That antibiotic mold turned out to be the fungus Penicillium. Over the next two decades, chemists purified it and developed the drug Penicillin, which fights many bacterial infections in humans without harming the humans themselves.

Penicillin was being mass-produced and advertised by 1944. Some remember World War II service members were advised to take the drug to rid themselves of venereal disease.

About 1 in 10 people have an allergic reaction to the antibiotic, according to a study published in 2003 in the journal Clinical Reviews in Allergy and Immunology; even so most of those people go on to tolerate the drug. That aspect, however, has been the impetus for the development of a large number of antibiotics. In a nutshell, Fleming's discovery over time has led to saving millions of people who otherwise would have died.

24. Contraceptives: Birth control pills and other forms of contraception have been a revolution; they have drastically reduced the average number of offspring per woman in countries where they reduce the number of people facing starvation. With fewer mouths to feed, modern families have achieved higher living standards and can provide better for each child. Meanwhile, on the global scale, contraceptives are helping the human population gradually level off; our number will probably stabilize by the end of the century. Certain contraceptives, such as condoms, also curb the spread of sexually transmitted diseases.

Natural and herbal contraception has been used for millennia. Condoms came into use in the 18th century, while the earliest oral contraceptive, "the pill," was invented in the late 1930s by a chemist named Russell Marker.

Scientists continue to make advancements in birth control, with some labs even pursuing a male form of "the pill."

A LONG WAY?

Looking back at these ground-breaking inventions, two things are clear.

Some people have a desire to improve and innovate. We see someone, usually a Lone Individual, and or with a Tonto or two who filled a need. So, they invented the wheel to tread the ground quickly, mastering the skies and waves.

This is truly remarkable and something that we could continue to do for ages to come if we face the enormous future challenges all of us together.

That, of course, leads to the question, will there be Lone Rangers to guide us through the morass surely to come?

Behind that question are two considerations. First, where and why have the Rangers failed, and what do they face as the future unfolds.

SELECTION OF RANGER REVERSALS

On this day, The Man began to turn Andrea and Triestan's attention to the reality of Human inhumanity, seemingly no matter the strength of the Lone Rangers.

Indeed, as a prominent example, following the "protective arguments" from various non-ranger leaders accepted by the masses the faiths, despite their foundational benevolent precepts, have led to the unbelievable killing.

 In telling of this, The Man did as usual, reading from references and shared pictures illustrative of the events from time to time.

Here he quotes: "A religious war or holy war " (Latin: *Bellum sacrum*) is a war primarily caused or justified by differences in religion. In the modern period, debates are expected over the extent to which religious, economic, or ethnic aspects of a conflict predominate in a given war.

 According to the *Encyclopedia of Wars*, out of all known/recorded historical conflicts (see following chapter), as many as one hundred and twenty-three had religion as their clear primary cause.

Although, the profound basis of the wars was complex, the outcome of killing based upon a given faith at times in history is a matter of record.

At this point, The Man provided a list for Andrea and Triestan to examine with a comment, this list shows those faiths with evidence of faith-based wars.

Examples Faiths Failing

Wars that carry a religious association with the cause

Africa
- Abrahamic–polytheist conflict
- Christian–Islamic conflict
- Inter-Islamic conflict (e.g., Sunni–Shia)
- Inter-Christian conflict
- Islamist or Christian fundamentalist insurgency against secular government

Americas
- Christian–Indigenous conflicts
- Mormon wars
- Inter-Christian conflict
- Christian fundamentalist insurgency against secular government

Asia
- Judaic–polytheist conflict
- Inter-Eastern religious conflict (Hinduism, Buddhism, Sikhism, Confucianism, Taoism, Shinto)
- Islamic–polytheist Arab conflict
- Islamic–Zoroastrian conflict
- Inter-Islamic conflict (Sunni–Shia)
- Islamic–Hindu conflict
- Christian–Islamic conflict
- Inter-Christian conflict (Catholic–Orthodox)
- Christian–Eastern religious conflict
- Islamic–Judaic conflict

Europe
- Inter-pagan conflict
- Christian–pagan conflict
- Christian–'heretic' conflict
- Christian–Islamic conflict
- Catholic-Orthodox conflict
- Catholic-Protestant conflict
- Inter-Protestant conflict
- Anti-Jewish pogrom
- Christian–secularist conflict

After all, studied the list The Man then said, "Examples can be cited for virtually every religious based faith or philosophy. From the list, however, I am only referencing a selection, others are fully cited in the account "History of Religious Wars."

Christianity

In early Christianity, St. Augustine's concept of just war (*bellum iustum*) was widely accepted. Still, warfare was not regarded as a virtuous activity, and there were expressions of concern for the salvation of those who killed enemies in battle, regardless of the cause for which they fought, which was expected. According to historian Edward Peters, before the 11th century, Christians had not developed a concept of "Holy War" (*Bellum sacrum*), whereby fighting itself might be considered a penitential and spiritually meritorious act. During the 9th and 10th centuries, multiple invasions occurred, which led some regions to make their armies defend themselves. This slowly led to the emergence of the Crusades, the concept of "Holy War," and terminology such as "Enemies of God" in the 11th century.

During the Crusades, those who fought in the name of God were recognized as the *Mellites Christi*, soldiers, or knights of Christ. The Crusades were a series of military campaigns during the 11th through 13th centuries against the Muslim Conquests. Initially, the goal was to recapture Jerusalem and the Holy Land from the Muslims and support the Christian -Byzantine Empire against the Muslim Seljuq expansion into Asia Minor and Europe proper. Later, Crusades were launched against other targets, either for religious reasons, such as the so-called Albigensian Crusade, the Northern Crusades, or political conflict, such as the Aragonese Crusade. In 1095, at the Council of Clermont, Pope Urban II raised the level of war from *Bellum iustum* ("just war") to *Bellum sacrum* ("holy war").

In 16th-century France, there was a succession of wars between Roman Catholics and Protestants (Huguenots primarily). These were known as

the "French Wars of Religion." Indeed, depicted by the famous painting, in 1572, the St. Bartholomew's Day massacred French Protestants at the hands of Catholics, as promoted by the Pope.

And, in the first half of the 17th century, the German states, Scandinavia, and Poland were beset by religious warfare in the "Thirty Years War." Roman Catholicism and Protestantism figured in the opposing sides of this conflict, though Catholic France did take the side of the Protestants, but purely for political reasons.

Islam

The Muslim conquests were a military expansion on an unprecedented scale, beginning in the lifetime of Muhammad and spanning the centuries, down to the Ottoman wars in Europe. Until the 13th century, the Muslim conquests were those of a more or less coherent empire, the Caliphate. After the Mongol invasions, expansion continued on all fronts for another half millennium until the final collapse of the Mughal Empire in the east and the Ottoman Empire in the west with the onset of the modern period.

There were also many periods of infighting among Muslims; these are known by the term Fitnah and mainly concern the early period of Islam, from the 7th to 11th centuries, i.e., before the collapse of the Caliphate and the emergence of the various later Islamic empires. The numbers of those suffering from these religious conflicts were beyond any sense of fundamental humanity or basic empathy in the religion.

While technically, the millennium of Muslim conquests could be classified as "religious war," it is essential to note the applicability of the term has been questioned. The reason is that the very notion of a "religious war" as opposed to a "secular war" results from the Western concept of the separation of Church and State. No such division has ever existed in the Islamic world, and consequently, there cannot be a natural division between wars that are "religious" from such that are "non-religious." Nonetheless, the conflicts were inter-mixed with the drive of those in the faith groups to rise to the top. They left vast numbers of people suffering over all time.

Judaism

In Judaism, the expression *Milkhemet-Mitzvah* or "commandment war" refers to an obligatory war for all Jews (men and women). Such wars were limited to territory within the borders of the land of Israel. The geographical limits of Israel and conflicts with surrounding nations are detailed in the Tanakh, the Hebrew Bible, especially in Numbers 34:1-15 and Ezekiel 47:13-20.

Due to the Jewish diaspora with Jews scattered worldwide living almost entirely outside of the Land of Israel, the concept of a religious war was absent in Jewish thought for approximately the last 2000 years.
Some assert that it may have re-emerged in some factions of the Zionist movement, particularly Revisionist Zionism.

From the earliest days of Israel's existence as a people, holy war was a sacred institution, undertaken as a cultic act of a religious community.

According to Reuven Firestone, "Holy War" is a Western concept referring to a war fought for religion against adherents of other religions, often to promote religion through conversion and with no specific geographic limitation. This concept does not occur in the Hebrew Bible, whose wars are not fought for religion or promote it but, instead, to preserve religion and a religiously unique people concerning specific and limited geography."

Israeli–Palestinian conflict

A demolished home in Balata, 2002, Second Intifada

The Israeli–Palestinian conflict can be viewed primarily as an ethnic conflict between two parties. One party is most often portrayed as a particular ethnoreligious group consisting only of the Jewish majority. It ignores non-Jewish minority Israeli citizens who, at varying levels, support an entire Zionist state. The minority is especially the Druze and Circassians, who volunteer in higher numbers for combat service. They are represented in the Israeli parliament in more significant percentages than Israeli Jews and some Arabs, Samaritans, various other Christians, and Negev Bedouin. The other party is sometimes presented as an ethnic group that is multi-religious (although most numerously consisting of Muslims, then Christians, then other religious groups), including Samaritans and even Jews.

Nevertheless, despite both parties' multi-religious composition in the conflict, elements on both sides often view it as a religious war between Jews and Muslims. In 1929, religious tensions between Muslim and Jewish Palestinians over Jews praying at the Wailing Wall led to the 1929 Palestine riots, including the Hebron and Safed ethnic cleansings of Jews. In 1947, the UN decided on partitioning the Mandate of Palestine, leading to the creation of Israel and Jordan annexing the West Bank portion of The Mandate.

Since then, the region has been plagued with life taking conflicts. Thousands have been displaced or killed in multiple bombings and rocket attacks.

Both Jews and Palestinians make ethnic and historical claims to the land, and Jews make religious claims.

The Nigerian Conflicts

Inter-ethnic conflict in Nigeria has had a religious element. Riots against Igbo in 1953 and the 1960s in the north were said to have been sparked by religious conflict. Riots against Igbo in the north in 1966 were said to have been inspired by radio reports of mistreatment of Muslims in the south. A military coup d'état led by lower and middle-ranking officers, some Igbo, overthrew the government. Prime Minister Balewa, along with other northern and western government officials were assassinated during the coup. The coup was considered an Igbo plot to overthrow the northern dominated government. Northern troops launched a countercoup. Between June and July, there was a mass exodus of Ibo from the north and west. Over 1.3 million Ibo fled the neighbouring regions to escape persecution as anti-Ibo riots increased. The aftermath of the anti-Ibo riots led many to believe that security could only be gained by separating from the North.

In the 1980s, severe outbreaks between Christians and Muslims occurred in Kafanchan in southern Kaduna State in a border area between the two religions. The 2010 Jos riots saw clashes between Muslim herders against Christian farmers near the volatile city of Jos, resulting in hundreds of casualties. Officials estimated that five hundred people were massacred in night-time raids by rampaging Muslim gangs. In recent times the Boko Haran, a radical Muslim sect, has held females; usually, young girls' hostage, and in-process have caused the revolutionary killing.

If the history of the various religious rooted peoples is carefully investigated, the labours of the original "Lone Rangers of Behaviour" have been deflected by many people to create "Spirit Wars." Preventing this there have been also "Humanitarian Lone Rangers" in insufficient numbers!

THE OFTEN VERY HIDDEN LONE RANGER

There are, of course, many that could be called forward to identify as Lone Ranger. Even in the conflicts outlined above, some often tried at the cost of their life to stop the insanity. It is that the events of history mask so many.

The following cites just one example. The reader is made aware that there are many others (and they may find it instructive to seek them out).

The following is the story of Ida B. Wells.

She was born in 1862 to slave parents who along with the rest of the slaves were freed in 1865. At 16 years, Ida's parents and older siblings died in the yellow fever epidemic. Here the first of Ida's courage came forward as she obtained a job as a schoolteacher and alone supported her younger siblings.

Ida Wells when she could move her family to Memphis, Tennessee. There she experienced the racism still prevalent when a "first-class ticket" she bought for a lady's car on the train was refused, and she was told to move to the colored car to make room for a white man. She fought back when the conductor tried removing her. " He caught hold of my arm; I fastened my teeth in the back of his hand." It took two more men to drag her off the of the conductor and off the train.

Wells sued the railroad company; she won the case in lower courts but lost the appeals in Tennessee's Supreme Court.

The case instigated the fight for equality. She became the co-owner and editor of the "Free Speech," an anti-segregationist Memphis newspaper, and focused her energies on revealing the horrors of lynching. In her book, "A Red Record: Tabulated Statistics and Alleged Cause of Lynching in the United States," she showed how horrifyingly common the practice was, picking apart on popular excused to justify it: A black man's rape of a white woman. "Somebody must show that the African American race is more sinned against than sinning. In the time of significant racism, she argued that rape defense was brought into a lynching case; the truth was that it usually was a voluntary act between a white woman and a black man. Wells traced the history of this rape defense and pointed out that white slave owners would often leave for months when leaving their wives under the care of their black male slaves. She noted white–black sexual liaisons were typically the other way around, with white owners sleeping with or raping female slaves.

Wells (again in a very, very difficult time) was the first to unearth the hypocrisy behind this so-called protection of white woman's honor through lynching; "To justify their barbarism." She wrote further, "they assume chivalry they do not possess... no one who reads the record, as it is written in the faces of the million mulattoes in the South, will for a minute conceive that the southern white man had very chivalrous regard for the honor due the woman of his race. Wells continued to work against racism with her husband, the writer F.L. Barnett until she died in 1931. She was a founding member of the NAACP and the first president of the Negro Fellowship League.

Racism in the United States continued, even though there were the times of Martin Luther King. It was only in July 2021 that the statues of Robert E. Lee and other Civil war south generals were removed from public places and colored Americans all continue to face cruel pressures from the citizens of right-leaning political thought.

One example of the often-hidden lone rangers was just given.

Even so, there are a great many in a group seldom considered. That is the women! Of course, each one raising children, with all of its many challenges, working alone in their families are indeed Lone Rangers- helpers for the future.

Since the beginning of modern humans, males have dominated societies. Major religions have all been male-dominated and misogynistic. But, in the 21st-century, women are finally achieving some equality with men in recognition of their contribution. Regardless, there have been many women who gained significant influence and contributed significantly to history. Following (with no bias intended) is a brief selection of these Women Lone Rangers.[1]

In ancient Greece, the Athenian philosopher Aristotle portrayed women as morally, intellectually, and physically inferior to men; saw women as the property of men; claimed that women's role in society was to reproduce and serve men in the household; and saw male domination of women as natural and virtuous. The Greek historian Herodotus expressed his astonishment that women could inherit, purchase and own property and slaves in Egypt and make legal contracts, all they could not do in ancient Greece. Herodotus records that there even was a female pharaoh, Hatshepsut, who ruled for 20 years in the 15th century BCE and was responsible for some of Egypt's prominent architecture. And the Greek female writer Sappho (6th century BCE) was recognized by Plato as one of ten great poets of that period.

In the Middle Ages, women who became too uppity were branded by church leaders either as whores or witches, as was Joan of Arc. There were a few exceptions, courageous women who strived above the

1.This section is adapted from the "Biega Information Treasure Chest."

entrenchment, for example, Elena Cornaro Piscopia (1646-1684), a Venetian noblewoman. She was the first woman ever to receive a Ph.D. (Philosophy). Marie Crous (birth date unknown) was a French mathematician. She introduced the decimal system to France in the 17th century and was frequently quoted in later mathematical works.

Prominent women rulers. Through marriage or motherhood, or as their father's heir, royal women occasionally rose above their culturally restricted roles when there were no sons. But it required supreme talent and effort to command male-dominated kingdoms. Empress Theodora (500-548 CE) was one of the most influential and powerful women in the Early Middle Ages. She was the wife of Emperor Justinian I and joint ruler of the Byzantine Empire. Theodora participated in making Constantinople one of the world's most sophisticated cities and promoting women's rights. She had bridges, aqueducts, and churches built. One such building, the Hagia Sophia, built between 532 AD and 537, is considered one of the most outstanding examples of Byzantine architecture. She had laws passed that prohibited forced prostitution and closed brothels. Theodora also gave women more rights in divorce and property ownership. She gave mothers guardianship of their children. Eleanor of Aquitaine (12th century) is renowned in the history books; she became Duchess of Aquitaine in her own right while she was still a child, then later queen consort of France (1137–1152) and then England (1154–1189). She participated in the Second Crusade, is also credited with promoting troubadours to sing tales of courtly love and chivalry of knights. Maria Theresa succeeded her father as empress of Hapsburg, controlled lands of Central Europe in 1740 and ruled until 1780. She brought about many economic and political changes to her empire. She made education mandatory. And "Mean" Queen Victoria 1837-1901. Despite massive politics, she supported a bill in Parliament which abolished slavery in 1838 throughout all colonies in the British Empire. She supported the "Factory Act," which reduced working days to ten hours. She influenced members of Parliament who passed the Married Women's Property Act in 1870. This act allowed the wages and earnings made by a wife to be held by her separate use; a wife was allowed to keep any property she inherited as her own.

Fight for Women's Rights. In the 18th. Century "Enlightenment," otherwise known as the "Age of Reason," spread throughout Europe from France; it aimed to reform society using reason. Nonetheless, Mary Wollstonecraft (1759-1797) was the only woman who could achieve prominence in the movement, a true pioneer in the struggle for female suffrage. She wrote a book, "A Vindication of the Rights of Women." This period ended with the French Revolution, in which women achieved equality only in the right to be imprisoned and guillotined whenever accused of disagreeing with the leaders.

In the 19th. Century, many more women gained prominent roles either as reformers or artists and scientists, although they gained it in grudging and often resentful acceptance by male-dominated organizations. There are among the great women fighters for reform the following.

Susan B. Anthony 1820-1906 - campaigned against slavery and promoted women's and worker's rights in the United States. Millicent Garrett Fawcett (1846 - 1929) was a leading suffragist and campaigner for equal rights for women in Great Britain. And Emmeline Pankhurst (1858-1928) was a British fighter for the right to vote even though she was jailed many times. Emily Howard Stowe (1831–1903), a Canadian physician, advocated for women's inclusion in the medical professional community and was the founder of the

Canadian Women's Suffrage Association. Raden Ajeng Kartini (1879-1904), was a Javanese (Indonesia) activist for the education and emancipation of women and abolishing the Muslim practice of polygamy.

Unfortunately, despite all the suffragettes' efforts and the time they spent in jail, the male political establishment did not allow anything to happen until the next century.

19th Century Accomplishments. Although the fight for voting rights made little progress in the 19th Century, little by little women gained improved property rights, the right to education, first in elementary and secondary schools. By the end of the century, most universities in Europe and the Americas were admitting women.

During the 18th and 19th Centuries, the role of women in economic life had also changed. Previously, their employment outside their own home had been limited to nannies, governesses, maidservants, on the farm, and in the making of textiles and sewing of clothing (particularly for women and children). In many eastern countries' women had traditionally worked on looms for the making of carpets as well as textiles.

Industrialization had broadened their opportunities, particularly in the rapidly expanding textile mills. But at the same time, their working conditions had worsened, being forced to work for long hours in dangerous conditions. Nonetheless, strong-willed women made progress in the fields of science and medicine. Among the most prominent: Ada Byron Lovelace (1815-1852) the first-ever computer programs were written by the daughter of the poet Lord Byron for use in the Babbage computing engine. Marie Sklodowska-Curie, 1867-1935 - the discoverer of radioactivity, winner of two Nobel prizes. The first woman to be appointed full professor at Sorbonne (University of

Paris) in 1906. Sofia Kovalevskaya (1850-1891), born to minor Russian nobility, was not permitted to study in Russia; in 1869, she traveled to Germany. There she was admitted on an exceptional basis to the University of Heidelberg to study mathematics. In 1874 received a Ph.D. *summa cum laude* from the University of Göttingen (Germany) and was the first woman to be appointed full professor, 1889 at the University of Stockholm. She received awards for her papers on differential equations and the mathematics governing Saturn's rings.

Caroline Herschel (1750 – 1848), born in Hanover (Germany), accompanied her musician brother Wilhelm to England. When he started building telescopes and studying stars, she assisted him and soon became an astronomer in her own right. In 1786 she discovered a comet named after her. Later she discovered several more comets and cataloged the stars. In 1828, she received the Gold Medal of the Royal Astronomical Society, the only woman to do so for another 168 years.

Elizabeth Blackwell (1821-1910) was the first woman to receive a medical degree in the United States in 1849 at Geneva Medical College (now part of N.Y. Upstate Medical University). She was also a pioneer in promoting the education of women in medicine. In 1857, together with her sister Emily, who had also obtained a medical degree, and Dr. Marie Zakrzewska, she expanded her original dispensary into the New York Infirmary for Indigent Women and Children.

And of course, there is Florence Nightingale (1820-1910), who enrolled as a nursing student at the Lutheran Hospital of Pastor Fliedner in Kaiserwerth, Germany. She then accompanied the British Army to Crimea (1853), where she set up field hospitals emphasizing hygiene, reducing the mortality rate by 60%. Upon return to England, she received a significant award from the British Government. She decided to use the money to fund St. Thomas' Hospital in London, and within it, the Nightingale Training School for Nurses.

In **the arts**, several women writers achieved success, although in the early 19th century, several of them used male names to be published at all or be treated seriously. Among them: The Bronte sisters, Charlotte, Emily, and Anne (1818-1858), did not reveal themselves as the original authors until several of their novels - *Jane Eyre, Wuthering Heights*, and others, gained popularity in Great Britain and North America. George Eliot, (1819-1880), (Mary Ann Evans) British novelist used a male pen name to ensure her works were taken seriously is best known for *Middlemarch* and *Mill on the Floss*. In France, George Sand. (Aurore Dupin; 1804-1876) first became an essayist for the Paris newspaper *Figaro*, then wrote several novels. She was an ardent socialist.

Other prominent and influential women writers of the 19th Century included Jane Austen (1775 – 1817), the first widely acknowledged British woman novelist. Her books, including *Pride and Prejudice, Sense and Sensibility*, realistically highlight the dependence of women on marriage to secure social standing and economic security.

Harriet Beecher Stowe (1811-1896) is best known for her antislavery novel, *Uncle Tom's Cabin*, which profoundly affected people's thinking in the northern states before the Civil War. She also wrote nine other novels and essays. And Hannah Adams (1755-1831), the first professional woman writer in the United States, wrote history books.

20th Century Accomplishments. The efforts of women activists finally resulted in obtaining the right to vote in country after country. Most remaining countries followed in the next 25 years; notably, France did not allow women to vote until 1944.

The efforts of women to assist their compatriots in two World Wars, working in industry and fulfilling essential roles in the armed forces of their countries, played a significant part in achieving recognition of their capabilities physical and intellectual. Consequently, by the end of the century, laws guaranteeing their equality with men had been passed in most major countries. By the end of the century, women had been elected in large numbers to the legislative bodies, participated in governmental bodies, and occupied significant executive positions in major corporations. True, their numbers in essential positions were still much less proportionally than the number of women in the lower ranks of these same organizations and much lower than the approx. 50% of females in the overall population.

For example, the number of elected women representatives approached 50% in only three countries in the year 2000:

Nevertheless, the situation is continually improving. During the 20th Century, 46 women had served their countries as president or head of government (prime minister). Some of them multiple times; for example, Sirimavo Bandaranaike, Sri Lanka Prime Minister, (1960-1965, 1970-1977, 1994-2000); Gro Harlem Brundtland, Norway Prime Minister (1981, 1986-1989, 1990-1996).,

Although no woman has served as President of the United States, 17 women served as elected governors of various states in the 20th century. And Kamal

Harris became Vice President of the United States in 2020, beyond which accomplishment she pioneered anti-racism, herself being of mixed race.

Running for a significant public office can be dangerous, particularly for a woman. Benazir Bhutto was twice elected Prime Minister of Pakistan (1988 and 1993). She was the first woman to be elected to any significant office in a Muslim country. In 2007 she was running for the third time and was assassinated two weeks before the election.

Aung-San-Suu-Kyi spent 15 years in house arrest because of her opposition to the military government of Myanmar (Burma). She was less severely treated because she is the daughter of a national hero who was assassinated in 1947 during the fight for independence. She was awarded the Nobel Peace Prize in 1991. In 2008 she was awarded the U.S. Congressional Gold Medal while she was still imprisoned. After the relaxation of the military government in 2011 and her release, her party won 81% of the seats in parliament.

Women still earn less than men in equivalent positions, but women have achieved equal rights through mostly their own heroic, lone (ranger) achievements in most countries.
Until a few years ago, women were notably absent from positions of C.E.O. or C.F.O. in significant corporations. Yet the July 2013 issue of Fortune magazine listed 21 women as chief executives of the largest corporations, including DuPont, General Dynamics, Hewlett-Packard, IBM, Lockheed-Martin, Pepsico, Xerox. Added to this, Women have become anchor-persons on many prominent television and radio news programs.

Even in predominantly Muslim countries, the situation is slowly improving. Since the year 2000, women have been elected to prominent positions in several such countries - president in Indonesia, two consecutive prime ministers in Bangladesh, president in Kyrgyzstan, prime minister in Senegal. Women have been elected to parliament in predominantly Muslim Afghanistan, Algeria, Bahrain, Bangladesh, Bosnia, Iran, Iraq, Kuwait, Pakistan, Saudi Arabia, Syria, Tunisia, Turkey.

The battles and the heroism of women so often acting alone continues.

Young women are fighting for their rights but still encounter great difficulties and are often attacked by extremists. A good example is the heroic Pakistani girl, **Malala Yousafzai**, shot in the head on a school bus in 2012 by a Taliban gunman.

Flown by the Pakistani government to England, she was miraculously saved. She continues to campaign for education for all children everywhere and has become a worldwide recognized example of courageous resistance to extremists.

WHAT THE LONE RANGER WILL FACE?

The point in all the above, female or male, rangers of invention, rangers of ideals, those with ideas for saving many humans, all those presented, is this. There have been many Lone Rangers in history in varied "disguise," but the ongoing troubles of humankind well into the current century have not been resolved. And added to this is, of course, the crucial question. *What does the Lone Ranger have to face in the Future?*

The record is that a selection of humans has arisen as Lone Rangers to help in this-that or the other situation, but the overall record is that humans are in a mess. To those that have helped so far, deep gratitude is given to them; they are very daring Lone Rangers. There are, however, situations that new Lone Rangers will need to ride into. This includes some 12 things most likely to destroy the world[1].

A new report claims to offer "the first science-based list of global risks with a potentially infinite impact where in extreme cases all human life could end." Those risks, the authors argue, include everything from climate change to super-volcanoes to artificial intelligence. By "infinite impact," the authors- led by Dennis Pamlin of the Global Challenge Foundation and Stuart Armstrong of the Future of Humanity Institute- mean risks capable of either causing human extinction or leading to a situation where "civilization collapses to a state of great suffering and does not recover.

~~~~~~~~~~~~~~~~

1.This section is adapted from the overview writings by Dylan Matthewsdylan@vox.com Feb 19, 2015. Images used were *via Getty Images.*
~~~~~~~~~~~~~~~~

Pamlin and Armstrong are, it seems, of the view that humans have a long time left — possibly millions of years: "The dinosaurs were around for 135 million years, and *if we are intelligent,* there are good chances that we could live for much longer," Roughly 108 billion people have ever been alive, and Pamlin and Armstrong estimate that, if humanity lasts for 50 million years, the total number of humans who ever live is more like three quadrillions.

That's an optimistic assessment of humanity's prospects, but it also means that if something happens to make humans go extinct, the moral harm done will be immense. Guarding against events with even a small probability of causing that is worthwhile[1].

So, the report's authors conducted a scientific literature review and identified 12 plausible ways it could happen:

1) Catastrophic climate change

The scenario that the authors envision isn't 2°C (3.6°F) warming, of the kind that climate negotiators have been fighting to avoid for decades. It's warming of 4 or 6°C (7.2 or 10.8°F), a truly horrific scenario in which it's not clear humans could survive.According to a 2013 World Bank report, "there is also no certainty that adaptation to a four °C world is possible." Warming at that level would displace vast numbers of people as sea levels rise and coastal areas become submerged. Agriculture would take a giant hit.

1. They also write, "Have we so far been intelligent about our preservation?" In the book "The Final Boundary, ISBN 978-0-46-46530-8," a clarification is made that there is a boundary to extinction. It is broad, but a complete examination argues that we are within the boundary facing the final edge.

Pamlin and Armstrong also express concern about geoengineering. In such an extreme warming scenario, things like spraying sulfate particles into the stratosphere to cool the Earth may start to look attractive to policymakers or even private individuals. But the risks are unknown, and Pamlin and Armstrong conclude that "the biggest challenge is that geoengineering may backfire and simply make matters worse."

2) Nuclear war

The "good" news here is that nuclear war could only end humanity under extraordinary circumstances. As the US bombings of Hiroshima and Nagasaki in World War II, limited exchanges would be humanitarian catastrophes but couldn't render humans extinct.

Even significantly larger exchanges fall short of the level of impact Pamlin and Armstrong require. "Even if the entire populations of Europe, Russia, and the USA were directly wiped out in a nuclear war — an outcome that some studies have shown to be physically impossible, given population dispersal and the number of missiles in existence — that would not raise the war to the first level of impact, which requires > 2 billion affected," Pamlin and Armstrong write.

So why does nuclear war make the list? Because of the possibility of nuclear winter. That is, if enough nukes are detonated, world temperatures will fall dramatically and quickly, disrupting food production and possibly rendering human life impossible. It's unclear if that's even possible or how big a war you'd need to trigger it, but if it is a possibility, that means a massive nuclear exchange is a possible cause of human extinction.

3) Global pandemic

As with nuclear war, not just any pandemic qualifies. Past pandemics — like the Black Death or the Spanish flu of 1918 — have killed tens of millions of people but failed to halt civilization. The authors are interested in an even more catastrophic scenario.

Is that plausible? Medicine has improved dramatically since the Spanish flu. But on the flip side, transportation across great distances has increased, and more people live in dense urban areas. That makes worldwide transmission much more of a possibility.

Indeed, this is the scenario with the Covid 19 Pandemic of 2020. The solution is for everyone to obtain vaccination using the unique RNA technology that scientists (Yes, Lone Rangers) have provided. Nonetheless, likely, millions will eventually be killed through the ignorance and selfishness of some.

Even so, a pandemic that killed off most of humanity would surely leave a few survivors who have immunity to the disease. The risk isn't that a single contagion kills everyone; it's that a pandemic kills enough people that the rudiments of civilization — agriculture, principally — can't be maintained, and the survivors die off.

4) Ecological catastrophe

Mass extinctions can happen for several reasons, many of which have their categories on this list: global warming, an asteroid impact, etc. The journalist Elizabeth Kolbert has argued that humans may be in the process of causing a mass extinction event, not the least due to carbon emissions. Given that humans are heavily dependent on ecosystems, both natural and artificial, for food and other resources, mass extinctions that disrupt those ecosystems threaten us as well.

5) Global system collapse

This is a vague one, but it means the world's economic and political systems collapse, by way of something like "a severe, prolonged depression with high bankruptcy rates and high unemployment, a breakdown in normal commerce caused by hyperinflation, or even an economically caused sharp increase in the death rate and perhaps even a population decline."

There are other possibilities, like a coronal mass ejection from the Sun that disrupts electrical systems on Earth.

That said, it's unclear whether these things would pose an existential threat. Humanity has survived past economic downturns — even massive ones like the Great Depression. An economic collapse would have to be considerably more massive than that to risk human extinction or to kill enough people that the survivors couldn't recover.

6) Major asteroid impact

Major asteroid impacts have caused large-scale extinction on Earth in the past. Most famously, the Chicxulub impact 66 million years ago is widely believed to have caused the mass extinction that wiped out the dinosaurs (an alternative theory that blames volcanic eruptions). Theoretically, a future impact could have a similar effect.

The good news is that NASA is reasonably confident in its ability to track asteroids large enough to disrupt human life upon impact seriously, and detection efforts are improving. Scientists are also developing ways to deflect asteroids that would have a truly devastating effect, such as by crashing spacecraft into them with enough force to change their path, avoiding Earth. (The dependency here, of course, is that some other catastrophe has not killed the space agency's ability to send up a destroying rocket.)

7) Super-volcano

As with asteroids, there's historical precedent for volcanic eruptions causing mass extinction. An example is the possible distribution of ash from a month-long Yellowstone super-eruption. The Permian–Triassic extinction event, which rendered something like 90 percent of the Earth's species extinct, is believed to have been caused by an eruption.

Eruptions can cause significant global cooling and can disrupt agricultural production. They're also basically impossible to prevent, at least today, though they're also extremely rare. The authors conclude another Permian-Triassic level eruption is "extremely unlikely on human timescales, but the damage from even a smaller eruption could affect the climate, damage the biosphere, affect food supplies, and create political instability."

As with pandemics, the risk isn't so much that the event itself will kill everyone so much as that it'd make continued survival untenable for those who lived through it.

8) Synthetic biology

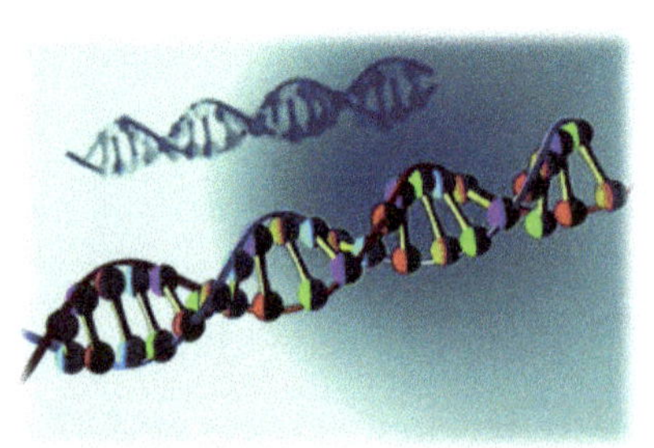

What if we tweaked this, so it killed everybody?

This isn't a risk today, but it could be in the future. Synthetic biology is an emerging scientific field that focuses on creating biological systems, including artificial life.

The hypothetical danger is that synthetic biology tools could be used to engineer a super-virus or super-bacteria that is more infectious and capable of mass destruction than one that evolved naturally. Most likely, such an organism would be created as a biological weapon, either for a military or a non-state actor.

The risk is that such a weapon would either be used in warfare or a terrorist attack or else leak from a lab accidentally (as some suspected was the case for Covid 19). Either scenario could wind up threatening humanity as a whole if the bioweapon spreads beyond the initial target and becomes a global problem. As with regular pandemics, actual extinction would only happen if survivors could not adapt to a massive population decline.

9) Nanotechnology

This is another potential risk in the future. The concern here is that nanotech democratizes industrial production, thus giving many more actors the ability to develop highly destructive weapons. "Of particular relevance is whether nanotechnology allows rapid uranium extraction and isotope separation and the construction of nuclear bombs, which would increase the severity of the consequent conflicts," Pamlin and Armstrong write. Traditional balance-of-power dynamics wouldn't apply if individuals and small groups were capable of amassing large, powerful arsenals.

There's also a concern that self-replicating nanotech would create a "gray goo" scenario, in which it grows out of control and encroaches upon resources humans depend on, causing mass disruption and potentially civilizational collapse.

10) Artificial Intelligence

The report is also concerned with the possibility of exponential advances in artificial intelligence. Once computer programs grow advanced enough to teach themselves computer science, they could use that knowledge to improve themselves, causing a spiral of ever-increasing superintelligence.

If AI remains friendly to humans, this would be an excellent thing indeed and has the prospect of speeding up research in various domains. The risk is that AI has little use for humans and destroys us all out of malice or perceived necessity.

11) Future bad governance

President Obama speaks about climate change at the UN, a perfect case study in the inability of global institutions to save humans from themselves.

This is perhaps the vaguest item on the list — a kind of meta-risk. Most of the problems enumerated above would require some kind of globally coordinated action to address. Climate change is the most prominent example, but in the future, things like nanotech and AI regulation would need to be coordinated internationally.

The danger is that governance structures often fail and sometimes wind up exacerbating the problems they were trying to fix. A policy failure in dealing with a threat that could cause human extinction would thus have hugely damaging consequences.

12) Unknown unknowns

The first 11 items on the list are risks we can identify as potential threats worth tackling. There are almost certainly other dangers out there with grave potential impacts that we can't predict. It's hard to even think about tackling this problem, but more research into global catastrophic risks could be helpful.

So, where does it all point to? Throughout history, horrible, senseless, cruel killing and torment of humans has occurred. This is so often the opposite of the main objective for them---the preservation of their species.

Heroes came along even from the earliest of times, trying to hold back the tide of things that were not good for humans.

From time to time, they succeeded in that, but all around them, human forces conspired to reverse the progress. The deep vicious side in the persona of Homo sapiens arose too often such that today humanity faces terminating challenges that could have had protective buffers and potential early solutions.

The pitfall is obvious, and humankind could have held all the negative back if but every one of them behaved as Lone Rangers.

That is the Lone Ranger that should have been is potentially already in all people. The means to achieve that is clearly in education; the way children are raised. They must be confident of their abilities, free of mind not to succumb to False Rangers, and with this hold, all minds centered on the purpose of advancing all people.

In a few words, the new Lone Rangers must be Future Navigators!"

LONE RANGERS NEEDED SOON

On this day with "The Man", Triestan commented right away, "Whew, there are some pretty big worries in front of us!"

So, The Man asked Andrea, in light of that, I see in your expression a question forming. Andrea then stands up and looks intently at the two. "First, a clear observation. In all of that we have seen, it is clear that there were not enough people to back the Lone Ranger, or to put it differently, there were not enough people being Lone Rangers!"

"And further, in all of this you have read-it says we must disagree with a fixed idea. There is nothing that insists that Leaders should be some charismatic exalted creatures. Those that try to fix this or that should indeed be honored. But all of us have that ability! It is just not recognized, not widespread enough. We can and should all be Lone Rangers, all supporting those that first enter to begin our defense."

Looking at The Man, she says, "I see you are holding "Navigating Forever, A Compass for Generations to Come"[1]; I have read it, and we, Triestan and I understand. I believe he will be, as each of us must be a Lone Rangers, Future Navigators. He will be raised to be self-actuating. And I see him digging into principles of the mind that will make him inciteful, independent of dogma, always seeking the balance and the truth, yet knowing all people are necessary and he is there for them."

Then, The Man looks at them, a loving look hugging her and waving his hand goodbye, he walks down the hill, disappearing toward the street! Triestan looks at his aunt and says, 'Auntie' I heard it, didn't you?

He said **Hi-Ho-Away!**

What about YOU?

See what Andrea learned and intends using as Triestan is raised in

The "CORE PRINCIPLES"[1].

(next page)

1. ISBN:9781034535058, https://www.blurb.com/b/10614356-future-navigation-hard-cover

THE CORE PRINCIPLES

Mature what you have read into the simple fact that none of the tragedies none should have occurred if the human has within these several characteristics well developed.

1. Firm self-reliance developed through lessons on life requirements and living techniques when rising to adulthood. That is, in a word being "self-actualized."

2. Security in their centered- free minds, fully capable of seeing truths and wrongness against fellow humans.

3. Awareness of the reality that we humans are those with the opportunity to be the superior species of the cosmos.

Further, every human being should have embedded the characteristics of a Lone Ranger to use that ability when the time comes to defend humanity.

Humans have developed an initial sense of morality, redemption, empathy, and broad humanitarian sensitivity. Preserving these senses and natural growth toward becoming the magnificent creatures they could be maintained in each new generation. Unfortunately, these senses have not been sufficiently realized so that each person works to secure the species.

To rely on one person, this one or that one as "The Leader, no matter what, as is so often the case, has given a record of history threatening to degrade our long-term survival. There are, however, a set of principles that will create more contributors to rational survival behavior.

Underlying the preservation and optimal growth for these characteristics are three fundamental ideologies: Protect, Develop, and Secure. The following are descriptions of these idealities.

A. PROTECT EVERY CHILD

Irrational wars, starvation, belief-based crimes, greed against children threaten our future. Therefore, we adopt a manifesto of values and behaviors uniting the highest doctrines of humankind into a "Final Code of Conduct." This is a system by which our children will survive in peace, happiness, and productivity for all the future. The method begins with the following recognitions.

1. That no dogma in faith should demand converting, dominating, injuring, or killing a "non-believer."

2. That political or national doctrine is used to harm any person is a crime against humankind.

3. That children will not be used as monetary capital for any reason. Wealth means returning love to them.

4. That murder is an act of insanity; persons committing this crime will be isolated from the population.

5. That religious belief based upon values and behaviors best for all human beings is taken without prejudice.

6. That every child should know that humanity is their family above all sects, states, or nations.

7. That every adult person contributes an act to support planet Earth and residence in the Cosmos.

From Earth's model, if needed, we will move all into and find ways to reside in the broader Cosmos, to create Earth-like places, "Tera-Realms."

8. All governments will be guided as the first principle by this; anyone who injures or kills a child commits a capital crime against the species.

9. That every government shall codify these principles in the laws of their nation.

10. We vow to the upbringing and education of all children as enumerated following.

1.) Every child will be guarded and supported to the most satisfactory health and education from birth at every place on the planet. We recognize that any child could be the seed of the "Final, Perfect Ultimate Human." So, all will be given a chance to mature in a safe and supporting environment.

2.) We will begin all our actions by never removing hope from any child! We recognize the line between hunger and anger is thin. Universal education of the world's children cannot occur in a world at war. We will work exhaustively to prevent the loss of young lives through starvation or in conflicts of idealism. Complete removal of war will be the goal of each person on this planet.

3.) Each day, we will honor the following practices born in the faiths and philosophies over humankind's history.

Islam: From the faith of Islam, we adopt the following. Children have the right to be fed, clothed, and protected until they reach adulthood. They must have the respect to enjoy love and affection from their parents. They have the right to be treated equally concerning their siblings in terms of financial gifts. Parents will provide adequately for children an inheritance. Children have the right to education. A saying attributed to Muhammad relates: "A father gives his child nothing better than a good education."

Christianity: From the Christian Faith, we adopt the following. Train a child to respect this idea "He will do unto others as he would have done to ones-self."

Judaism: From the Jewish Faith, we adopt and will hold the following. Girls will be given the same level and quality of education and the same rights as boys.

Buddhism: From the teachings of the Buddha, we will hold the following. We support our children to become generous, compassionate, virtuous, responsible, skilled, and self-sufficient beings. We will give them the necessary mental skills they need to find true happiness. To that, the most important thing is helping them to understand that every action has consequences. Each of those actions will determine their happiness, not only in the present but in the future. That is the fundamental lesson of karma, or cause and effect.

Hinduism: From the Hindu belief, we consider the following. One should discover and explore spirituality, religion, and God on one's own, and that we shouldn't interfere. It's okay to share and teach. It's another to misuse God to strike fear in others.

Pantheism: If you choose to believe in a god, hold that personally without others' evil intent. Recognize that each faith's prophet would have the same God's direct message; there would be no other choice, one believing in one God. In this, there is thus no reason for a polemic. However, above all, rest in the beauty of the world into which you were born, so sympathetic with your existence, in that alone is the unification of all faith. Stand unified in those ideas, the same God, the same creations, your precious Earth.

Atheism: From the Atheist, we pay attention to the following. Early implantation of religion should avoid damage in the following ways because children are especially vulnerable to mental harm related to it. This includes extreme guilt about normal, healthy sexual functions, disrespect for science and reason, feeling warlike toward others who do not hold the same faith. Remember, free inquiry on all matters strengthens the species.

B. FURTHER TO THE PROTECTION OF CHILDREN

We will help children along the path to self-control. That means they grasp reality, the karma of their lives. That means understanding things as they are and realizing the truths of life, seeing things through, and grasping the impermanent and imperfect nature of worldly objects and ideas. Since our view of the world forms our thoughts and our actions, this view, developing self-control, yields the right thoughts and actions for all people.

Children will be guarded such that they grow into self-actuation. For them will be available to discover- be educated with a higher sense of purpose, realizing the Cosmos is for our species a provided ideology because they are first Cosmos-lings! As they view this future, we will help them to understand that Earth is their glorious ark. It must last for thousands of generations. In its beauty, we have matured in the naturalness of Earth's sympathy for our species.

Children will be informed as to the matter of how our species is improving. We have become aware that of all the species, our strongest suit is our ever-maturing brain. Our species plan is to continue that remarkable development. This means that their Brain DNA in transferring and improving through the living generations ensures the arrival of "Ultimate Humans." The young will be provided with insight into this so that they may respect it as adults.

We will teach our children to join in the mission of feeding all the world population. Sapiens can mobilize to go to the moon; the same species can certainly mobilize the world's children's proper feeding in every corner. The young should have complete insight into this as the charge of all humans when adult!

Children will be informed about the conflicting forces that create behavior. The brain-driven urge to destroy is an embedded part of the fittest's survival, yet that drive refers to the physical and, with self-control, can be managed. The brain-driven urge of benevolence is also embedded. It is that drive that referees the preservation of the species. It is our strongest suit, the ability to think things through. The young should have complete insight into this as a principle to reflect upon when adults.

Children will be allowed and guided by example into ethical and mental self-improvement. That is, resistance to the pull of desire, opposition to feelings of anger and aversion, and not thinking or acting cruelly, violently, or aggressively, and developing compassion. This education will avoid proselytizing children into beliefs for which there is no substantiation.

We will teach the young that their children will be the next form of their species, the path to the future, and full enlightenment. To aid children in each new generation, adults will learn that natural development, as described by Maslow, creates self-activating humans. This means that as adults, they will take responsibility for their reproduction. Wise and considerate human pairs will inevitably beget wiser ones. And children will grow up without female victimization by men.

C. SECURE HEALTHY GROWTH

The buffer and the guide to develop healthy-minded humans in each generation is to respect that they have a psychology of needs!

Respect for this development in the face of damaging cyberspace, proselytization, and political influences will produce more secure, self-actuation persons.

The human mind is complex and different motivations can occur variously over lifetimes. However, they can be arrayed much as in a pyramid, although each person from their starter knowledge may experience these differently, some in sequence, others some aspects may coincide. Nonetheless, the fundamental transition in growth to adult to be respected is described by the psychologist Maslow (in a "Hierarchy of Needs").

Physiological needs. Physiological needs are the physical requirements for human survival. If these requirements are not met, the human body cannot function properly and will ultimately fail. Physiological needs are crucially essential; they should be met first. Air, water, and food are metabolic requirements for survival in all animals, including humans. Clothing and shelter provide necessary protection from the elements.

Safety needs. Once a person's physiological needs are satisfied, their safety needs take precedence and dominate behavior. In the absence of physical safety – due to war, natural disaster, family violence, childhood abuse, etc., people may experience post-traumatic stress disorder or transgenerational trauma. In the absence of economic safety due to financial crisis and lack of work opportunities, these safety needs manifest themselves in ways such as a preference for job security, grievance procedures for protecting the individual from unilateral authority, savings accounts, insurance policies, disability accommodations, etc. This level is more likely to be found in children as they generally have a greater need to feel safe.

Safety and security needs include personal security, financial security, health and well-being, And a Safety net against accidents/illness their adverse impacts.

Love and belonging. After physiological and safety needs are fulfilled, the third level of human needs is interpersonal and involves feelings of belongingness. This need is powerful in childhood, and it can override the need for safety, as witnessed in children who cling to abusive parents. Deficiencies within this level due to hospitalism, neglect, shunning, ostracism, etc., can adversely affect the individual's ability to form and maintain emotionally significant relationships in general, such as Friendships, Intimacy, and Family.

Humans need to feel a sense of belonging and acceptance among their social groups, regardless of whether these groups are large or small. For example, some large social groups may include clubs, co-workers, religious groups, professional organizations, sports teams, and gangs. Some examples of small social connections include family members, intimate partners, mentors, colleagues, and confidants.

In capsule, humans need to love and be loved by others. Many people become susceptible to loneliness, social anxiety, and clinical depression without this love or belonging element. This need for belonging may overcome the physiological and security requirements, depending on the peer pressure's strength.

Inherent in this is the social grouping that arises from cyberspace, for example, dangerous, such as suicide groups or terrorist organizations. Social networks should provide warnings and options to bring individuals

Self Esteem. All humans need to feel respected; this includes the need to have self-esteem and self-respect. Esteem presents the typical human desire to be accepted and valued by others. People often engage in a profession or hobby to gain recognition. These activities give the person a sense of contribution or value. Low self-esteem or an inferiority complex may result from imbalances during this level in the hierarchy. People with low self-esteem often need respect from others; they may feel the need to seek fame or glory. However, fame or glory will not help the person build their self-esteem until they accept them internally.

Psychological imbalances such as depression can hinder the person from obtaining a higher level of self-esteem or self-respect. Most people require stable self-respect and self-esteem.

The psychologist Maslow noted two esteem needs: a "lower" version and a "higher" version.

The "lower" version of esteem is the need for respect from others. This may include a need for status, recognition, fame, prestige, and attention.

The "higher" version manifests itself as the need for self-respect. For example, a person may require strength, competence, mastery, self-confidence, independence, and freedom. This "higher" version takes precedence over the "lower" version because it relies on an inner competence established through experience.

Deprivation of these needs could result in an inferiority complex, weakness, and helplessness.

Self-actualization. "What a person can be, they must be." This quotation forms the basis of the perceived need for self-actualization. This level of need refers to what a person's full potential is and the realization of that potential. This level is expressed as the desire to accomplish everything that one can, to become the most that one can be. Individuals may perceive or focus on this need very specifically. For example, one individual may have a strong desire to become an ideal parent. In another, the desire may be expressed athletically. For others, it may be expressed in paintings, pictures, or inventions.

Self-transcendence. The above staging in life was set down by A.H Maslow, who wrote on "The Hierarchy of Needs." Maslow explored a further dimension of needs. *The self only finds its actualization in giving itself to some higher goal outside oneself, spirituality or altruism, and helping others.*

This involves Transcendence, a state that is a critical plan applying to the ever-increasing and inserting "Global Brain."

"Transcendence refers to the very highest and most inclusive or holistic levels of human consciousness, behaving and relating, as ends rather than means, to oneself, to significant others, to human beings in general, to other species, to nature, and the cosmos."

Open-Mindedness is an essential component in such mature growth. It is a release from dogmatic thinking. Children will then be better prepared to "Self-Actualize" and ready to contribute to societies, benevolent and robust development,

D. INSURE OPEN-MINDEDNESS

Open-mindedness is essential to maintain humanity's sense that will derive from child protection and growth development programs. The protected, mature individual will resist the aberrant influences in cyberspace and other intrusions in rational thinking. Over generations, from parent to child, the idealized will bring humankind into a star reaching Nirvana.

Following are steps in mind development for individuals (and addressed to them) to help Mind liberated growth. These are the ideas that are central to the mental calm and clear viewpoints of those among us who wish to help guide us to the future, the Future Navigators.

E. **PRINCIPLES FOR THE MIND**.

1. <u>Understand Chaos.</u> We live with a sense of Chaos, but if mental calm occurs - patterns can become aware. New thoughts are generated. We can gain clearer insight. The following helps in removing the sense of Chaos.

2. <u>Know Dream Reality from Possible Reality</u>. There is an edge to reality. We are often unable to grasp it. It is as if truth exists over a razor's edge. Thus, we live in the dream of immortality. Be calm, realize it, there is the reverse side to everything, and know that even the reverse has a reverse- these we may never be able to see. So, then you are back to the only possible reality for your day today, the present you! ***Your <u>mind</u> is that which governs your existence!***

3. <u>Respect the Cosmos.</u> Remember, the Cosmos and our World are older than us. We are at the end of a long chain of responses; whatever we do, Cosmos has a head start! Reality proceeds, yet the direction we (you) set

may be a part of that! If you try, and try again and fail, the Cosmos is speaking to you. If you feel successful, you are in the possible process!

4. <u>In Thinking Gain Freedom.</u> Freedom and security are interdependent, yet we grow by separating these two (in our minds). Security has a definite minor connotation. Freedom has an immense and unlimited sense. Behind security, there are boundaries; when we can cut through them, there is freedom. Freedom from boundaries puts one within an understanding of how their lives fit within the Cosmos. The mind cannot expand unless the center is preserved. That is achieved by selecting wise boundaries. With incomplete or arbitrary boundaries, the whole structure endangers collapse. An intelligent center allows for delightful freedom. (Protecting the center of one's mind; makes it a capable mind, then the future has the potential to be protected.)

5. <u>Protect Your Mind.</u> *The preciousness of your mind is impossible to underestimate. Use it or be abused by it!*

6. <u>Make A Capable Mind.</u> The cause is given meaning by your noting the effect carefully! Know then that a single event is a tunnel through which all events reflect. These two causes and effects cannot be separated. You learn to understand them, first in the minuscule, which leads one to understand the most important macro. *In bees, it is the multifaceted eye in humans; your capable mind can see that you see!*

7. <u>Overcome Interrupted Mind.</u> The mind is full of noise, contributing to that sense of Chaos. Focus until it quiets to a single sound! Then will occur but one voice. Silence frees one from the interfering internal dialog!

8. <u>Overcome Troubled Mind.</u> Some have developed a library in their head that becomes but one book, in their view, the "Truth Book." The one-book mind attempts to avoid becoming contaminated by outside ideas. This one-

book mind is a system with such firm boundaries that it leads to defending self, then to bigotry and wars!

9. <u>Realize the Difference Between Belief and Freedom.</u> Belief takes meaning into formalization, then fossilization. However, if understanding is allowed to shift, each thought can be a path to freedom.

10. <u>Believe Just First in Everything.</u> Much of the conflict between people is from colliding beliefs. So, practice believing initially in everything! Yes, that sounds strange, but internally, in time, the parts will sort logically, leading to one big idea, hence, no boundaries! The absence of boundaries should free one from the desire to be always right (which most of us have). Significant problems can be solved, sometimes by evaluating the wrong. One should rather be happier in ideas that can be improved than fearing the wrong.

11. <u>Allow Time to Grow</u>. Focus on nature; it has much to say. Remember the message in the seeds. Your time will come, and with it, a time to grow!

12. <u>Understand the Difference Between Fear and Courage.</u> Fear is controllable. If you think about it, we only fear what we "see" in the future. The rest is anticipation. In fear, we begin to imagine what we can't do rather than what we can. Dwelling on what you can't do leads to fear; concentrating on what you can do leads to courage!

13. <u>Know Change and Learning Are Interlocked.</u> To learn is to change; to change is to learn. There is no learning without change! To remain unchanged is to stay forever without comprehension.

14. <u>Understand Perception concerning Reality</u>. We must accept that there are both perceptions and reality. More aptly put, more relevant to us as persons, human life is "Attending." We can't turn it off. It is always pointing at something as long as we are feeling we "Attend."

15. <u>Recognize the Modes of Attention.</u> Within our attending, there are four modes: External and Internal, Narrow and Wide. We exist or see existence in one or the other. Learn to know the whole! When looking down, also look up, expand the narrow to the vast and vice versa. *Your choices at any time depend on the extent you see!*

16. <u>Expand Attention to Its Twelve States.</u> Contract and magnify as you observe; use your attention! To add sparkle to the world, practice alternate meditation, knowing each mode well at first. It is recognized that there are 12 states of awareness: three senses; sight, hearing, touch, and four modes; internal, external, wide, and narrow to achieve 3x4 states. In your Mind gain, switch from external to internal using each. This will help your mind to become richer, more mature!

17. <u>Know the Basis of Behavior and Perception</u>. We don't disagree over what we perceive (usually). We often disagree over what those perceptions mean to us individually! Thus, the behavior may be the person; how we respond gives the behavior meaning. The response is a secondary feeling, an emotion! The original perception is the primary or internal feeling. *To un-bias yourself, change your sense of perception variously.*

18. <u>Balance Change and Response.</u> Responding to change can create meanings, thus giving you choices and access to different worlds. Changing response lets one see the world as an opportunity! This is what we call an "Open Mind."

19. <u>Enhance Attentions.</u> Practicing each, so it grows, makes perceptions big enough to evaluate. The distance will lead to improved attention, enhancement, and more excellent value. *In effect, become a "Mind Tracer."*

20. <u>Learn Translation.</u> Learn to "Translate" each state. Make light have feeling, and rock have fragrance. Intelligence is limited by the number of

states one cannot master in this way. The more this can be achieved, the richer is the life experience. Translation helps to join one in existence within the Cosmos. In unhappy situations, one shifts attention through this means to relieve pain or boredom.

21. <u>Move External to Internal.</u> A skilled Mind Tracer shifts attention, external to internal, to achieve their skill. They see an external and envision its meaning internally, which means appreciating the mental processes. There are two; "Defining" and "Exploring." Too much-defining leads to narrow judgment and views, but it can be helpful if balanced. It may lead to more fruitful exploration. If one starts with the basics of looking for something, they may find something even more enjoyable. Pioneering something in this way for a group means the pioneer may gain unprecedented freedom, a unique feeling of accomplishment!

22. <u>Know Type of Questioning Relates to Happiness.</u> The essence of the Human is to understand, to be attentive. So, how questions are asked is essential. When we question, we should use the 12 states to enjoy, this to wander, this to let the ordinary become extraordinary.

Even so, the words used are pretty important. "Why" is a question of dogma, leading to more Whys? "Why" questions sometimes work but don't necessarily lead to information particularly useful because this is thinking virtually, totally about meaning. "How" questions are those with a more often helpful basis. One is thinking about actions. "How" leads us to use our senses probing into time, space, weight. We see the Cosmos as phenomena, take advantage of the universe's action on itself to accomplish! Our essence, our mind, turns wishes into use. We are excited about this skill. The skill at this is the measure of your life. It's very much about "How"!

23. <u>Grasp Importance of Context in Thinking.</u> "Content," "Reality," and "Timing" only have meaning within the "Context" that they belong. These are subordinate to Context. Therefore, our ideas about them are changeable. These should be viewed within their specific diversity to arrive at an accurate understanding of them. We should first want to understand that process, even though the outcomes become what is desired.

24. <u>Understand the Basis of Feelings.</u> Feelings prompt a "Human Fog." There are two parts. Primary feelings are those of warmth, pain, satisfaction, the actual world. Secondary thoughts are the emotions and responses, the meanings we apply. They are how we think about the world. These can be and are most often mistaken, intermixed. Feelings mixing with emotions can lead one astray. We must evaluate whether the information is appropriate between the two. Knowing the difference leads to better decisions.

25. <u>Calculate Connections.</u> Dreaming or envisioning is not a place, but it is the process of calculating connections between points. The insight comprehensively gained is in using the twelve states.

26. <u>Recognize and Use Space in Mind.</u> The mind has the property of space. Space is not just something to fill casually. Space can be thicker or thinner depending on how much has gone to matter. So, mind space has tremendous power and promise! *When stretched to a new dimension, the mind is never the same; it is now accepting new matter (ideas recorded).* To receive something new, one must "empty some mind space," then open the door and let the future in; endless possibilities can come from this!

27. <u>Avoid Depression, Madness, and the Lost States.</u> These things happen when one has lost the RANGE of attention, i.e., the twelve states. They are not out of mind but lost in a limited realm within it. Perceptions are fixed! The mind is safest, not locked in, but when one is exploring freely within it.

To discover and reveal hidden inner riches is the most exhilarating work of all!

28. Realize Differences: Religion Vs. Science and Self. Religion can deflect one's attention inward in a virtue versus failure appearance to God, i.e., one is to behave in a certain way, making them hostages in a sense. Science directs one's attention outward. One becomes an aggressor for making change. In a sense, when over-consuming awareness, both fail to strengthen the individual as they abandon "Self-Regulation." One to be happy self regulates oneself, mind, body, and spirit. Once internally sound, one can then go out to see if that changes perception. Without self-regulation, peace can only happen in a perfect world and must fail. Anything the mind can't seem to affect must be external. Oscillate between the exterior ideas in relation to your foundation of internal strength!

29. Know the Promise of Human Maturity. "When one resides within a correctly dimensioned drum, the sound of a beating heart is greatly magnified" … "When one truly sees the magnificence of human possibility, the sound of future beating hearts amplifies one's own! Humankind has incredible potential, but only if it continues to exist!

30. Seek Aging Well. The body sends strong messages to the old. To respond with courage, recognize time is the one resource you have. Manage it well. Here, the most important thing is your voice. Learn that even now, so what you say is heard. Complete is each day doing! Incomplete is unfolding! Blend these, and the beauty of life unfolds. I am. Am I? Complete, Incomplete. With time ahead, you are incomplete!

31. Guide Yourself Internally. Wanting to be perfect begins with self-control internally. We think of the past as influencing what we should or should not do. Talking to yourself in the right way can ease the stresses

produced by this. You have "Mind Police" built up in your raising and experience. These are what others want you to do, but you take control by your voice. Remember to change the "You" voice to the "I" voice. Internal You leads you to some statement about yourself, usually in the wrong way. "I "-needs never to tag negatively. With "I," you can change to the positive such as "I want to share my success." Cease wanting to be perfect by the Mind Police's demands, give that up and stay with the good myth about yourself. That way, you avoid living in "a Police State." Relief is then gained. Delight is felt when your internal voice wins.

32. _Change Yourself-Upward_. With each heartbeat, we are changing. Time is the master. All our "Life Waves" are sums of our simple waves, compiling (tangled rubber strings by simile, Item 43). So how do we best change ourselves, take control of the waves? Emphasize the "I" voice; drop you "always will be." That is *with the "I" voice you gain; in effect, you control time. The "You" voice plants you in the past.* Ignore it. Emphasize the wonderful. *The "I" voice directs you to your future.* The mood is set by who is talking in your head. Be free of your past, the Mind Policing; it only continues to affect you.

33. Expand the Right "Mind Code." Pronouns (as above) are the way the mind addresses itself. However, look at the mind as a verb; it is what the brain does! The brain's memory is in Chaos, and the brain itself is a combination lock for everything. These things can be brought up in several ways; one word will evoke several meanings. Being dumb allows just one door to open from the Chaos! Being smart is allowing multiple doors to open. Make a Mind Code for something important to you, anything stored or just hanging there, then bring it back and expand it. Once a bit of the Chaos is trapped (put in order), let it gather new thoughts!

34. <u>Know Limits in Existence.</u> Your life exists only in your mind! Unhappiness is sure to follow if your view of what the world is fixed (such as the perfect religion, the ideal car, move, etc.). *View the world as incomplete, with room to finish it.* Knowing your mind leads to understanding your body. This gives the marvel of reducing illnesses that limit you.

35. <u>Know What Is Complete and What Not.</u> For strong-viewed people, the world is fixed, so every discussion is a fight or an attack. If thoughts are reopened for the debate, the world is open to many things. By knowing not to complete, minds are changeable. Each can make this discovery, and a wonderful world results. Remember, "It depends, also depends." We search for new places when we have "transformed eyes."

36. <u>Solve Problems and Issues.</u> No matter how big or small, the approach to every problem can be mastered by an expansive process in your Minds-Eye. First, take the situation and expand it to as large a field as possible, organizing it into a single picture in your mind. Then rise above that picture to look down on it and *arrange* the pieces. Now the clearer picture can be made smaller and then lower toward you. When small enough, insignificant actions become coordinated beauty and might are created! The brain's random neural discharges must be linked and combined before the magic of thought and understanding appears!

37. <u>Apply Superior Meaning.</u> Wrongly, values and beliefs become the lens through which we look and color how we see the world. This turns infinite into finite! Instead, *see the world as incomplete and possible.* Practice finding several meanings to each situation. The "this and that" events should not yet have real meaning. First, see without seeing "Meaning"; attempt to

see what is! Once the big pictures are manageable, stay with that optimal, adjusting slightly as needed.

38. <u>See Together the World from Your Mind.</u> Nothing is completed in the world unless it is completed first in your mind. Once mastered, know what you can do and don't know what you can't do! There is no time when self-reliance wouldn't be an asset. But seek people you can complement while avoiding those with whom you are weaker. In the beginning, these "Seeking's" may be muddy waters, but even muddy waters can quench a fire!

39. <u>Draw Opinions from Different Views.</u> The mind operates differently among different people. Thus, the far northern people see the top and bottom of things (sun rising and falling, only). The equatorial sees the left and right sides of things (Sun rotating east to west). Remember that while we see much the same (it is the same sun), there are differences in how different minds see the world. *Draw opinions from different views to gain your strength*!

40. <u>Recognize You Can Change Ideas or Concepts.</u> Your mind is potent. One can use it to help oneself change almost anything, from pain to strange notions. There are two ways of remembering 1.) "As it happened to you," and 2.) "As you see it happening, removed from you." When it is "attached," you feel it "Here"! When detached, you are at a distance from the pain or idea. Suppose you run it back from that distance. In that case, you can find ways to control it until you get to the attached to be rationally evaluated.

41. <u>Change Limits to Perfections.</u> The mind can do anything through imagination; you can even envision more extraordinary imagination. In that

state, you have the model! Knowing it well and with a method, what you can do is unlimited. Many institutions will not accept the unlimited. They think it is dangerous and set boundary places in children. However, humans are born to fight over limits. The space in your mind can determine what the world will be. It is born in you. One always wants to be correct, sometimes making one confused. Remember through the newly activated space in your mind. Sometimes more perfect things can be made out of air!

42. <u>Seek the Unknown.</u> Behind almost everything, there is the reverse, or the hidden, beyond your immediate vision. (Below the plant are the roots). It is also an energy that can be seen sometimes, worth the effort when one develops deep inner vision. It can give you power for an exceptional journey. Ask! Use your imagination; that is the tie-in to power. What you can compute may not seem achievable, but you know you can do it!

43. <u>Understand Time Truths.</u> Life can be compared to a rubber string, lengthening in time, along the way tangling, tangles representing trials, successes, and progeny making again more tangles. When thoroughly taught the life string, let's go, snapping, releasing energy, returning to the original state, and the energy is provided to one following. (Matter will by us, neither be created nor destroyed, only return to energy.) This is a natural phenomenon. *You have though control of the tangles, the balance that creates or destroys them. So, to do your best in life, recognize and balance destinations.*

44. <u>Be Wise in Destination Choices.</u> The best lived lives see and understand destinations clearly. Choosing destinations involves two

activities, 1.) Comparing, 2.) Contrasting. These are 1.) What someone wants you to do, choosing it or me, for example in religion, or 2?) What you want to do. Comparing is using value differences, Contrasting is using exact measurement, no value implied. In Contrasting judgment is made considering things as parts without meaning. Comparing is "the difference between it and me," contrasting is "the difference between it and It." If there is much emotion, one is comparing; if not, one is contrasting. As destinations are sought, one asks, what is the meaning in knowing this (compare), or what is the difference between these options (contrast)? One's delight is the measure of whether they are in proportion with these two, whether they are centered rationally within their Minds-Eye! That also means one strives for simplicity in life, not determined by imitation of others.

45. <u>Find Your Center</u>. When analyzing "Space" filled with objects, the objects seem uneven, but there is a center to a flowing river. We can compute it but never really see it. One's mind is full of boundaries, but there is a center. If one understands the ideas herein, one can find one's center. At the center is a surprise – a source of happiness, a sense of rest!

46. <u>Understand Feelings</u>. Each of us has primary and secondary feelings. Moods are secondary feelings, which are either attached or hanging detached.

These feelings are similar to our two nervous systems, i.e., voluntary, involuntary. For example, we see a mountain. It is fixed, high with color, angles, and dark canyons. This is the "Content Code," the involuntary. It is there. The way we see it is voluntary. This is the "Mood Code."

These two give our thoughts "Meaning." If we are afraid of heights, we may see an ominous fearful structure.

If we have a different Mood Code, we may see the beautiful purple in the mountains' evening light. The Mood Code can be other than ominous; it can be changed, so can the memory of things.

47. <u>Understand How to Use "Meaning."</u> From feelings, we develop "Meanings" to events and things. All meanings are arbitrary, one's interpretation. The meaning of anything is the way we represent it in our Minds. Meaning has the power to connect the Mind and Body. For example, emotions (meanings) can be registered and affect our bodies. If one changes the meaning ascribed (for example, it's a lousy world), that will change how one feels. Changing another's meaning could change the world!

Meanings are guided by the constraints of our history, often making things difficult. However, if we change the meaning toward the obvious in front of us (finding order out of Chaos), all else can be automatic. The obvious is the law, for which there are real consequences (what you do now can affect what happens to you in the future).

If using "You" the "and" says you are damaged, then you are a different person, a damaged one. Conversely, if "I" is used, you can change your perception of yourself and become un-damaged. Suppose one connects the two halves of the brain (the obvious to the consequences). In that case, there is enjoyment in understanding direction, a sense of delight happens!

48. <u>Recognize the Flavor of Reality.</u> Although we have mood and content codes, we may have different moods, depending on what content we see or know. We can change the character of reality and how we feel about it

despite the Cosmic cause and effect. This is because the world itself has no meaning; without thought, we give it through the state of our Mood Code.

Part of how we see reality is entwined with "Anticipation." If we anticipate a loss, then we are in a state of anxiety. If we anticipate a gain, we are in a state of excitement. However, knowing that moods are coded, it isn't easy to complain. One needs to imagine how they would code to feel in an "Up Mood."

These comments are not to say the World is just "Made Up." Because we have limits, we can't argue reality per se, but we can adjust our thoughts to the "Flavor or Reality" with which we choose to live. One's life can be sour or sweet. It is a decision each can make despite the fixed cosmic cause and effect within one's mind, though how they reflect on the world - change in their life can occur.

People and institutions set themselves up to define the "Flavor of Life" and expect you to agree that is the way the world is. However, there is never an entirely correct answer. Although there are Cause and Effect "How" you deal with, it is your choice!

49. <u>Become A Decider.</u> In every journey, one hopes to reach toward the end. More than just being a "Doer", maturity leads one to become a "Decider", making the mind aligned and clear as described in this document on "Principles for the Mind."

The discourse you studied (this was a "Means" journey) now approaches that special point. The last means concerns becoming a Decider that is a Future Navigator, where one is helping others!

50. <u>Navigating Others into the future.</u> Minds gained through the "Means Journey" just taken can heal oneself and, indeed, the world.

Some final valuable recognitions, signposts with clear lettering, help toward cementing that goal.

What is needed so that one can (internal skills gained) externalize to be of value to others---the human species?

It first is essential that each person heals self. Then they can try and likely want to contribute to healing the world, as our humanity is built-in an inherent instinct!

The following aspects center upon that possibility. They are as follows,

A.) Controlling our memory's structure -how the past affects us.

B.) Controlling Time, and

C.) Understanding the Intersection of Imagination and Reality.

A.) <u>Controlling the Structure of Memory.</u> On the way to a healthy mind, one wishes to forget a "bad and frightening" experience. Indeed, space for wisdom is needed in our often too crowded Minds.

Some of the past, of course, amounts to lessons of progress and is retained in respect. Forgetting the unacceptable, the wrong, the cruel, the selfish, though it takes effort.

Still, we have direct control over how it affects us because we control memory structure, as we have learned. So, being enlightened, we know that fear can now be seen as an arbitrary-an internal event; the internal component can be controlled. Fixed, Mind Books can be re-written!

Control over memory means developing a simple set of priorities. These priorities tell us, in a nutshell, that we first mind our own business! We are capable of doing this when we are prepared to supervise our instruction without the usual boundaries!

One only needs to set priorities; self-determination- creates their future; avoidance of trends (that gives us quilt in the end), integrity—thus not regretting our actions. And control of the Central Core, i.e., the "Foundation of Self," is not restricted by useless boundaries.

B. <u>Controlling Time.</u> Being attentive creatures, or ones desiring to lead, the "Future" has a significant meaning, and in fact, offers pressure in our daily lives.

"Future" might be described as the consequence of present circumstances, making it in a sense static or limited. That is, to us, there are only two ideas of time. These notions are "ongoing" and "finished," which seem to "leapfrog" forever. They proceed and direct all our actions in a limiting game.

However, we have control by stepping back and simply asking, "What is ongoing? What is finished? We have the power to decide to turn these into "Now is Dynamic," "Then is Static."

The future is, thus, opened up to more possibilities.

We select successful past ideas and continue to explore them. We use our available tools to regulate thought about time. We recognize that to know one thing is to open the potential to know a thousand (if not today, then tomorrow). Well-practiced ability expects success with developing ability.

C. <u>Controlling Intersections between Imagination and Reality.</u> Controlling this intersection comes about when one grasps meaningful meaning.

In reality, give the world a chance; it will resolve everything (good or bad). One then recognizes that the world sits between one's "to be" and "to do." In that is the critical intersection; it is the one between imagination and reality! Our lives are within, i.e., between those "Spaces."

If you control yourself, then you control the environment between imagination and reality.

Such control is a seeming paradox, but in truth---one must first become self-centered in minding one's own business. And controlling one's internal environment achieves a healthy and mature state!

If your control of the mind is done right, then regarding others, you will ask, "What in this situation loves them and me?" If that were accomplished for each of us, there would be no reasons for conquest, conflict, or greed. We would all be safe in independence from each other, but by the same token, available as a success for each other!

That clearly has been the mindset of those who have been our Lone Rangers. They were in control of their minds and free to help others.

If your actions, when done this way, work well for you, they will fill you with delight! They will direct you to the "Something" for which you are looking.

They will become a self-correcting life map, and that will be work done without effort because work done in a pattern of joy is work without effort!

THE AUTHOR

Eye Mask off.

Dr. David Yourtee, Emeritus Professor UMKC, is the author of this book.

Such insight as shared with you comes from his experience on medical humanitarian missions as a Fulbright Scholar.

Included, and sincerely acknowledged, critical to the accounts are the referenced opinions of authors whose great wisdom is clearly evident!

The Lone Ranger? (**?** deliberate in title) is proceeded by the following books in the Future Navigator Series.

The Final Human, Future Navigators Arise, The Future Navigator, A Navigators Journey Through Time, Navigators on the Edge of Forever.

Important Navigator observations are in the books, The Omega Shield, Offspring, The Final Boundary, The Vistavien Agenda, and Navigating Forever. An important look ahead can be found in the volume The last of Us and the Earths' Future.

These books are published by Minds-Eye Manuscripts, LLC, Grand Junction, CO. Previews are available at **https://www.blurb.com/ bookstore** under the authors' name or by selection of the book on the store at **https://www.aminds-eyejourney.net/main-book-store**

Communications to Minds-Eye@bresnan.net are most welcome.

Becoming a Lone Ranger guarding the future will help ensure for the children of the world, their happiness, health and safety!

Every human being should have embedded the characteristics of a Lone Ranger to use that ability when the time comes to defend their fellow humans from untruths that lead to tragedy.

Every one of us should understand and practice centered and objective love and a protective instinct for all our fellow humans!